THE HIDDEN
TREASURES
WITHIN

Advance Praise for
The Hidden Treasures Within

"This wonderfully written book by Dr. Leonard Elkun is not a how-to book, as much as it's a road map of things we need to think about life, moving into The Third Age. It's obvious that this comes from the heart of a man with great insight. I know you will enjoy reading it as much as I did."
—Wayne Bourke

"This is an impressive book of essays on various aspects of the human condition by Dr. Leonard Elkun, a prominent Chicago psychiatrist and psychoanalyst. Dr. Elkun's extensive and wide-ranging clinical experience as well as his own aging process generated this book. It is written in a flowing easy-to-read style. There is much truth and wisdom in this work—especially the essays dealing with time management, sexuality, and death. I would highly recommend this book for professionals in the mental health field as well as lay people."
—Benjamin Garber, M.D.

"This book is an amazing, loving, wise book that will change the way you think. I love dipping into its pages and seeing a new or perhaps a clearer way of living, loving, and coping with the changes that happen as we get older."
—Dr. Susan Hiscock, Obstetrician and Gynecologist

"This book is a compelling look at the maturing process of later life through the eyes of Dr. Leonard Elkun. He has used his professional and extensive personal experience to give us a very important and stimulating book, allowing us to potentially maximize our happiness as we age."
—Ron Hunter

THE HIDDEN TREASURES WITHIN

ON WISDOM AND OTHER ESSAYS

LEONARD D. ELKUN, M.D.

Producer: aka Associates
Editor: Dana Elkun
Copy Editor: Robert Yates
Front Cover Design and Illustration: Timothy Foss
Book Design: Zaccarine Design

ISBN 13: 978-0-57822088-8
ISBN 10: 0578220881

Disclaimer: As with any personal growth book, readers are advised to use their own best judgment in using methods provided. For those working with significant life issues such as abuse or trauma, or in the event of any concern about whether or how to use these methods for yourself, we recommend contacting a skilled professional who is thoroughly trained in these methods for guidance. The information presented in this book is offered to you as a service. By reading this book you agree that you are responsible for any results of your decisions and actions relating to your use of the material presented.

DEDICATION

To Julia, my closest friend:

It's beautiful when you find someone
who is in love with your mind.
Someone who wants
To undress your conscience and
Make love to your thoughts.
Someone who wants
To watch you slowly take down
All the walls you've built up
Around your mind and
Let her inside.

I have been unbelievably lucky
to have found just that.

Table of Contents

Introduction xi
Editor's Note xvii

SECTION ONE: The Awareness of Aging

On Aging 3
On Time Management 9
On Success 17
On Retirement 23
On Creativity and Productivity 27
On Youth and Youthfulness 31

SECTION TWO: Relationships and Aging

On Knowing and Being Known 39
On Family 43
On Peace in the Valley 49
On Sexuality 53
On Marriage 61
On Grandparenting 67

SECTION THREE: Living and Letting Go

On Spirituality and Religion 73
On the Extreme 83
On Illness 87
On Last Goodbyes 93
On Inheritance 97
On Dying 101
On Wisdom 107

Index 113
About the Author 117

Introduction

The ideas behind these essays were initiated some years ago. For many years my good friend Ron Hunter and I met every Wednesday morning for breakfast at our favorite early-morning spot in Chicago. And while we changed locations periodically over the many years, this one restaurant remained our customary meeting place. We were mostly left alone by the owner of this little restaurant and by the wait staff because we must have seemed so engaged in stimulating conversation. And that was very true.

It was a meeting I looked forward to every Wednesday. When Ron was away on vacation or out of town on business, or when I was on vacation, whenever we would fail to meet, I would feel the absence of that important and intense connection to my good friend and to our dialogue.

In early 2001, Ron began contemplating the process of retirement from his important and relatively high-profile position in Chicago. While his actual retirement did not occur until fall 2002 and included a permanent move to Kentucky, he still returns to Chicago for one week per month, which always includes at least one breakfast together and often a dinner as well. His interest in planning for retirement decidedly changed our conversations, which began to take focus on psychological issues associated with retirement. For nearly twelve months it was our singular focus, opening up numerous questions for both of us, and we discussed these ideas with great enthusiasm and curiosity. At some point during the discussions the topic almost seamlessly broadened to issues associated with the whole aging process.

In communication with another friend, Terry Savage, who has written a number of successful books herself, I felt encouraged to write a book on how to retire successfully. I thought I would take up the question of what issues, psychological and otherwise, are problematic for people in that age group, and how one might overcome those obstacles to achieve a successful retirement. Terry was very supportive and helpful in promoting the idea that I could make this book happen if I wanted to. She also reassured me that the topic was important and timely.

In conversations with my Italian teacher, Stefano, we would periodically discuss my reluctance to put my ideas about this topic onto paper. His boundless enthusiasm and adventuresome personality prompted my willingness to try this endeavor. So at the same time as I was struggling with learning a new language, I was also trying (in Italian) to do some self-analysis on my resistance.

Throughout 2003 I made some attempts to begin this "how-to" book but found myself stymied and struggling. I realized in late 2003 that I did not want to write a book telling people what to do, what they should think about, or how to choose their futures. It goes totally against the grain of my basic ideology as a psychoanalytically oriented psychiatrist; I encourage people to come to their own conclusions and find their own directions through a process of self-exploration and discovery.

Also, in late 2003, I read Ralph Waldo Emerson's essay, "Self-Reliance," and I suddenly felt that perhaps I could use a similar format. Why not simply state the relevant issues as I understand them, particularly issues I felt were important to the whole concept of aging, and let people ponder the ideas themselves? I have not professed anywhere to having the definitive answers to any of the questions that have been raised. I simply want to stimulate thought in others. And particularly in others at the age when many of these issues seem so relevant.

On the first day of 2004, I wrote a New Year's Day email to my relatives and friends, suggesting that they all do something this year that they have wanted to do for some time, but for whatever reason (time, resistance, fear, etc.) they had failed to do so far. I realized I was also talking to myself. Once I got started, the writing happened with relative ease.

Clearly much time has passed since I set out to write this series of essays. As one can easily see, this journey began in 2001 with my friend's move toward retirement. And after a number of starts, I finally felt in 2004 that I had said what I wanted to say. I was always pleased with what had been produced.

A number of people, including my daughter, who edited this group of essays, would ask, "What do you want to do with this?" I never knew, and would say that the joy for me was in the writing, not in what I did with it, or whether it would have any kind of general distribution. That to gather my thoughts into some kind of cohesive grouping was satisfaction enough. Thus, the book sat on my shelf until now.

About one year ago, my cousin Paul called and told me that a psychologist friend of his had picked up the book buried in his magazine rack, read it, and was enthralled by some of the ideas. Paul prompted me: it had clearly been a substantial effort to organize my thoughts and to work with my daughter to pull the book together, so why not do something more with it?

My wife, who has infinite belief in my ability to think and write, has also been encouraging me to put this out to the public, perhaps to a more discerning public. "Why would you deny people the opportunity to think about these provocative topics?" I did not have an answer to her question. But an answer was necessary.

The prospect of sharing my personal ideas about life, and about aging in particular, showing people who I really am and what I really believe, seemed too exhibitionist, too narcissistic. But on closer inspection and self-reflection, my real hesitation was rooted in my age-old self-doubt. How could I believe that I had the clarity of thought, insight, discovery, and psychological understanding that would interest others?

But at age 78, if I really believe what I've written in these chapters about aging and the invitation to take chances courageously, to be open and not to keep score, why not release this book that I have harbored privately for almost fifteen years into the larger cultural dialogue? From this new vantage point, I could see absolutely no reason why the book needed to remain hidden in the darkness.

And so, I have undertaken the task of getting this creation of mine, of which I am very proud, into the open air. *The Hidden Treasures Within* reflects my broad-based understanding of psychological issues encountered through the practice of therapy. It brings a level of maturity, wisdom, and an in-depth understanding of the psychological vicissitudes of the human condition, common to all of us.

While this book is not a "how-to" book, nonetheless by reading it carefully, the reader will find hints and suggestions for finding satisfaction and joy in later stages of life. Knowledge obtained from this book requires the reader to do his or her own self-reflection and to question personal motivations and proclivities buried within.

My intention in writing these essays was solely to appeal to that part of you, the reader, that can and will reverberate with this material, and to encourage you to locate yourself in relation to the material. What you do with what you read and process is totally up to you. But I hope that going forward you will be stimulated to heighten your self-reflection and questioning and will more attentively consider your day-to-day behaviors. I also hope that you will be motivated to change your life where it seems fit to you and in connection with your goals for yourself, and that you will attend to the beautiful and precious moments of later life in a more pleasure-seeking and playful manner.

I truly believe, and even more so now that I have tried to articulate my feelings about the aging process, that we are capable, perhaps more capable than earlier in our lives, and certainly far more capable than we ever expected, of finding peace, harmony, happiness, joy, wisdom, creativity, and generosity within ourselves.

I fully expect there to be readers who disagree with certain ideas and personal attitudes that have slipped into these chapters, but that too is central to being human, i.e., to communicate and indulge the wish to be known and to know others. I welcome dialogue of all sorts, especially from points of disagreement. There are no better ways to learn and expand one's base of knowledge and understanding than through open discussion and the exploration of divergent opinions.

This life of ours, no matter how long we may have, is totally ours to live. So let's do it with gusto, enthusiasm, and respect for ourselves and others. Those of us currently in the midst of the aging process (not that we don't begin aging even as babies) find ourselves at a time in history when many of us can expect to live far longer lives than our parents or grandparents; we are likely to have the freedom and hopefully the energy and psychological resources to continue our self-development and evolution. And happily we are not in any particular rush to get anywhere! That's the beauty of later life and the reward that we have all earned for experiencing our idiosyncratic lives.

Keep in mind that no one is watching you, no one is grading you, and no one is keeping score. You don't have to keep score either. There is no winning or losing, only living well.

Leonard D. Elkun

Editor's Note

In 2004 when my dad and I first discussed the possibility of my editing his book of essays, I knew it was a rare opportunity for a daughter, a chance to witness my dad's worldview more fully and for my dad to witness the adult me more fully too. We spent about six months emailing drafts back-and-forth and discussing what kind of voice he wanted to capture in his book. The whole process was exciting and exposing, like climbing a mountain together. The farther we went, the fewer trees we found for shade or privacy. And the air was sometimes thin, rarified. But the views were stirring and beautiful, and we traveled well together.

Editing this book was a moving experience; it moved me closer to my dad and the sweetness of our adult friendship, but also closer to myself. Every chapter was another invitation to think through my emotional inheritance from my dad, to consider how I've melded that with other influences to become who I am, for the moment anyway, since the "self" is moving too.

Reading back over my dad's thoughts on aging, I feel his big-hearted spirit on every page. He has always wished for people around him to journey inward toward the self, and to live joyful, courageous lives. In fact, he has organized most of his life around those wishes, as a psychiatrist, but also as a father, husband, brother, cousin, grandfather, and friend. I offer my work on this book to my dad and his community with my love and gratitude.

Dana Elkun

THE AWARENESS OF AGING

On Aging

Man, how did it come to this? For a long time, I wasn't even slightly prepared or motivated to take on the question of aging. From early childhood on, I observed the process of aging in my parents, aunts, uncles, and grandparents with a certain lack of curiosity. After all, what did that have to do with me? I was still very young with decades upon decades left to live. So the process of aging was very far off in the future for me, as it is for most young people.

When I approached 60, the reality of aging began staring me straight in the face. It was not just the sagging skin around my eyes or the flesh that was over my belt no matter how hard I tried to suck it in; more importantly, it was the subtle changes I detected in my thinking and my approach to the world that confounded me. I don't mean a sudden preoccupation with death and dying, or a vision of my final days in the rocking chair awaiting my final moment. It was a slow and sometimes painful awareness of the passage of time and the inevitable loss of possibilities for the future. And that awareness becomes clear to each of us, no matter how much we have done or not done, how much success or failure we have experienced.

We have all heard that "time flies, especially as we get older." And while it's true that twenty-four hours for a 5-year-old is no different quantitatively than twenty-four hours for a 65-year-old, there is a substantial difference in the qualitative nature of that time. Simply because we know that time is drawing down, its passage is more acutely felt. And like good health, once it's gone, even for a short while when we suffer with minor illnesses, its value becomes that much more palpable. We resent spending even one day ill because of the increasing value of time. Such an important and irreplaceable commodity. When it's gone, it is gone!

I know that is no revelation to any of us. So why in fact do we become more concerned with the passage of time and the ways in which we use that time? Our increasing fixation on time may have to do with unfulfilled wishes for ourselves and for those near and dear to us. Every one of us suffers in this way; even the most successful among us entertained wishes about things we wanted to do with our lives that we never got around to or didn't fully pursue.

The awareness that time is "running out," however slowly and imperceptibly, leaves us with a panicky feeling. This feeling is related to the questions: "What will I leave undone?" and "What will my legacy be?" These core uncertainties are of great concern for many of us and generate a whole set of additional questions. What will the world think of me after I'm gone? What have I contributed to my immediate world, be it my family, community, or more extended areas of influence? How will I manage the time that remains for me? And how can I assure myself that I will accomplish or at least attempt whatever I truly want to achieve in the time left? Amid this cluster of questions is where panic can arise. If the list of things to do feels insurmountable, or the time remaining feels too short, a feeling of anxiety can easily emerge. Unfortunately, this anxiety will only create obstacles to further achievement, particularly if it becomes overwhelming.

All too often, both younger and aging adults look at aging as associated solely with loss; for example, loss of strength, loss of function, loss of usefulness, loss of self-esteem, loss of opportunity and options, loss of support, loss of contact, loss of productive work, and loss of hope. This absolutely does not have to be the case. Not even a little bit! In fact, the aging process is replete with advantages and opportunities. Sure, it's true that certain things will be very different for the 70-year-old than for the 40-year-old, but not as different as one might anticipate. If one remains focused solely upon physical aspects of life, the older person has lost much compared to the younger person. But aging offers unique opportunities for achievement that younger folks will have to wait a long time to experience or may never experience.

The best example in this realm is the acquisition of wisdom and cosmic understanding that can only come with age and reflection. Those who do achieve wisdom and understanding will enjoy rich rewards and gratification. To a certain extent, every person who reaches 60 years of age or older will already understand much about their particular universe, even if they cannot clearly articulate it. And they will be available to share that understanding with those who are open to receive it. This is a direct benefit of aging, albeit one that is often overlooked. This is not to say that wisdom and knowledge come to you magically as you pass your 60th birthday. Acquiring wisdom is a slow process, one that may start much earlier in life, but it surely ripens and deepens with age and reaches its most glorious phase later in life.

All too often we have been led to believe that old is obsolete. And we can thank the modern technological age for hastening and facilitating that perception. Isn't yesterday's computer old and useless today? Isn't the new cell phone today ready for the garbage dump tomorrow? All of this contributes mightily to the concept that old is useless, that youth is "where it's at." That idea may be one of the great misconceptions of our modern day. Too often we fail to see the information that can be extracted from past experiences. We are too quick to transition and change to something new when obstacles arise. Isn't it easier to simply replace than repair?

There is very little in our experience as young people that engenders a kindly approach to aging. We all know that young is beautiful and desirable, and if we need any reminder, we can consult any television advertisement. Who is selling the beautiful cars or furniture or clothes?

Nobody over 30 years of age. We are reminded daily and exhaustively that young, new, and shiny is in, and old, wrinkled, and tired is definitely out. So who wants to go there?

This line of thinking has had a deleterious effect on us all. Younger people often fail to take advantage of the experience that older people can offer, thereby depriving themselves of valuable information and input, and depriving their elders of the chance to contribute to the world around them. As such, it is no wonder that we approach aging with trepidation and denial. If to become old is to become outdated, unusable, out-of-step, immobile, out to pasture, non-productive, and uninformed, no wonder no one looks forward to old age with curiosity. No, thank you very much! If you don't mind, I'll put it off until much later. Or maybe I'll never face the issue of aging at all. Alas, we must all take a hard look at aging sooner or later. And the later we do, the less prepared we will be for the changes that inevitably "befall" us.

At a time when our population as a whole is aging and living longer, a growing percentage of Americans are in the older age groups and will remain so for a considerably longer time. With each generation, we live as part of the older population far longer than our grandparents did, but even longer than our parents did as well. So we must understand the struggles and joys of this dilemma. Those of us who refuse to address the issues may essentially miss out on golden opportunities to enjoy our remaining years in creative and fulfilling ways and to maintain a rich sense of self. Denial has never been an effective mode of adaptation, especially when dealing with inevitable change.

The aging process seems to encompass a variety of unknowns, but they are only unknowns because we are reluctant to consider them directly. And why are we so reluctant? Beyond the fear of various losses discussed above, and, perhaps more importantly, there is the looming question: "What am I going to do with my time?"

Some individuals enter (perhaps reluctantly) into a phase of retirement or semi-retirement for which they are inadequately prepared; after a six-month tour around the world, they fall into a depressive state. Other individuals retire from an active work life, which formerly provided most of their stimulation and gratification for many years, with precious few diversions in place; they can fall into a state of boredom and psychological exhaustion.

I believe that the single most effective way to ensure a successful transition into retirement and later life is for an individual to prepare for the future by considering how to manage his or her time. It is not simply a matter of having regular golf dates established with a group of friends, or regular fishing trips with the guys, or programmed vacations. If that were all it took, it would be fairly easy. Experience suggests that this transition requires careful and thoughtful consideration.

Because each one of us is so vastly different and receives stimulation and gratification from vastly different sources, we cannot follow some generalized "program for later life" and merely fill in the blanks, expecting a successful transition. Each one of us must tailor our own time and manage it in such a way as to provide the stimulation, self-esteem, intellectual challenge, physical output, gratification, and feeling of productivity that is idiosyncratic to our personality.

Unfortunately there is no formulaic way to age without careful self-evaluation, without learning what in your life excites you now and what has excited you in the past. Many of us have not yet discovered or recognized what truly interests us. We may not have given ourselves the luxury or time required for self-exploration and self-reflection. And yet it is crucial to know yourself if one day you are going to effectively manage your time without the structure of work.

While I do not think that this inquiry into one's self requires psychological exploration with a skilled therapist over many years, I do strongly believe that some consistent effort toward self-awareness needs to be developed. With effort, anyone can uncover clues within oneself that will reveal directions and interests for the future. This is often tied to significant and recurrent themes that have existed throughout a person's life but that go unnoticed over time. Becoming aware of those themes and then utilizing the proclivities contained within those themes can lead to effective time management and a more joyful aging process.

On Time Management

Perhaps the central thesis in all of these essays concerns the reach for effective time management. What I mean specifically by time management is the manner in which an individual thinks about time, plans for it, takes advantage of it, and derives maximum gratification from its passage. Generally, if we have ever considered this concept, it has principally been applied to carrying out one's workday. The term "time management" is used as a hedge against wasting time at the workplace. And certainly while work is one of the sites for effective time management, it is by no means the only one.

It is evident that the passage of time is critical during all stages of life. Needless to say, we adopt a rather loose and easy-going attitude toward time when we are very young. The passage of time is essentially meaningless, its measurement unnecessary. As children, time is what we fill with play and enjoyment. At a slightly later stage, perhaps beginning in the latency years, we are introduced to time in the form of school time, i.e., the stretch of hours when we are no longer playing freely or at our own direction.

Instead we are initiated into the experience of time being structured for us, with particular goals of productivity and learning associated with that structure. And while there is a wish from teachers and other adults that our structured time be pleasurable and stimulating because that facilitates learning, enjoyment is no longer the primary focus of time spent. Learning, creativity, and productivity become the focus. Thus, from very early on, the structuring of time may become associated with the giving up of freedom, particularly if it is structured in an imperious manner and without careful consideration given to the pleasurable aspects of that structure.

I cannot emphasize emphatically enough that the manner in which our time was planned for us very early on in life, and the degree of agency we had in altering plans to our liking, will largely determine future attitudes toward time management. For example, an overly structured child will grow to hate the rigidity of his time whereas an under-structured child can suffer with boredom and lack of stimulation and motivation, thereby growing to hate the lack of structure and the time he is forced to spend feeling aimless. Children who have been optimally structured (their time has contained adequate free play, they derive adequate pleasure from both free and structured activities, and they have had appropriate input into the specifics of that structure) will obviously have a far more positive feeling regarding management of their time in the future.

Much has been written about the over-structuring of children in America. There are so many options available to children that parents can overload their children with stimulating activities, each in their own way worthwhile, but without consideration for the extent that structured activities may interrupt a child's freedom to play and fantasize creatively. One can see how future time management will be dramatically influenced by the goals and priorities that parents and teachers set for children's utilization of time.

Children who have been overly structured from early on will not know or remember that they need time and space to play and think on their own. They may misconceive the intent of their parents or teachers and may even believe that free time is wasteful; and deleterious. They may learn early on that productivity is the only measure that matters, not enjoyment or self-satisfaction through work.

Furthermore, the children and later the adults who have acquired a firm conviction that productivity and praiseworthy outcomes are where true value and self-esteem come from will be painfully disappointed when their devotion to work (perhaps even at the expense of all other potentially gratifying activities) is not adequately rewarded by the world around them. And they will also discover that while their focus on productivity at work and perhaps also at play does not bring them the anticipated rewards, it may even bring them isolation and a lack of respect from the outside world. A rather bitter outcome for such intense effort.

Even more painful can be the growing awareness that self-esteem is not primarily derived from productive output. And how effectively will these adults manage their time when they find themselves with unstructured time without the usual methods of producing in order to measure themselves? Likely they will do poorly. What a depressing discovery to make later in life, that true feelings of internal worth and value are not measured by outcome, even though it sure seemed that way at the beginning.

The under-structured children and then adults will also be woefully unprepared for the effective utilization of their time. They will have been left too much to their own devices. They will likely have chosen one of two directions.

The first possibility is that because they lacked help in creatively structuring their time earlier on, they may remain unstructured and undisciplined, thus unable to apply themselves to any persistent activity, which leads to a markedly reduced capacity to generate positive self-esteem and self-satisfaction from their work or play life. If they have never learned to extract pleasure and positive internal feelings from their activities, they will likely not be motivated to creatively utilize their time in the future either.

The second possibility is that the under-structured children who have been left to their own devices may impose even more stringent and demanding goals for themselves. Because they had few guidelines from potentially helpful outside authority figures, they may significantly over-shoot the intensity of requirements for success and self-satisfaction, giv-ing themselves little or no latitude whatsoever with respect to play or pleasure-seeking. They will have imposed an extremely constricting set of internal guidelines for themselves. Perhaps these guidelines are so stringent that the possibility of deriving pleasure and gratification from any activity, no matter how successful they are, is totally absent.

In this case, the bar will have been set so high that satisfaction is never possible. These individuals will clearly have difficulty setting attainable goals for themselves later in life and will experience great stress in managing their unstructured time. Their tendency will be to return to overwork, over-productivity and overly restrictive patterns of time utilization, again eliminating the ability to have free, creative, and self-esteem enhancing play.

People talk often about the necessity for living in the here and now. Especially as we get further into the aging process, we understand more and more that life is lived right now, that to put things off into the future may well sacrifice the present, that this is the only life we have on this earth, as far as we know for sure, and that if we do not take advantage of the opportunities that life presents, we may lose that opportunity by wait-ing for a better time to act. How many times have we all heard the ques-tion, "If you were dying and you knew it, what would you do with your remaining time?" And then the follow-up questions, "Then why don't you do it now anyway, especially when you are perfectly healthy and able to do those chosen activities? Who knows what will come later?"

But there seems to be some resistance to actually "living in the present," even though we all pay lip service to the concept. Perhaps it sounds or feels too self-indulgent, too self-aggrandizing, too impul-sive. For whatever reason, we seem reluctant to stay focused on the present so we refuse, sometimes inexplicably, to give ourselves over to pleasure-seeking. And when I say pleasure-seeking, I do not mean reck-less, hedonistic, unbounded over-indulgence without consideration for appropriateness or reason.

We've all seen the bumper sticker on the car of an elderly person, "I'm spending my children's inheritance," and we can chuckle about the audacity of the sentiment. But how many of us would actually do it? Many of us have some deep-seated feeling of obligation to provide for our children in the future, and some of that impulse is very positive and valuable, but to the extent that we deprive ourselves in order to carry out that obligation may be unreasonable. And I would suggest that the resistance to living and enjoying now can be based upon deeper-seated, self-doubting phenomena.

There are individuals who are overly focused on reliving experiences and righting past wrongs, either that they have committed or that have been done to them. To the extent that they are "stuck" in the past in the hopes of rectifying these wrongs (primarily by magical thinking), they will be excluding themselves from life in the present. Whenever I think of this particular dynamic, I recall Dostoevsky's short story entitled "Notes from the Underground." Now here was a man who took himself right out of his life. He was totally preoccupied with an apparent slight that occurred some years earlier, and he could not move on without righting that wrong. He was so obsessed with this miniscule bit of his past that he was unable to focus on the present. If we believe that we must "fix the past" before we can move on, we can eliminate any possibility of gratification and participation in the present. This desire to fix the past is widely endorsed in society and can perpetuate exclusion from real living.

Then there are individuals who are overly focused on the future. They often feel that preparation for the future guarantees future satisfaction. By squirreling away money, time, energy, and interest for the future, we can take ourselves right out of life once again. I don't mean to imply that planning for the future is always disruptive; of course it has its place. However, when planning becomes what one does instead of living and enjoying, then it is counter-productive to life.

The polarities mentioned above, excessive focus on the past and excessive focus on the future, are out of place only when they push focusing on the present into the background. Some degree of focus on the past is enormously helpful. To analyze and learn from experience and to redirect oneself on the basis of what is learned is constructive, creative, and evolved. And progress cannot be made without some awareness and reflection upon past performance. It is only worrisome when that focus becomes obsessive and repetitive, motivated only by the wish to repair past hurt instead of learning for the sake of today.

Similarly, some degree of focus on the future is also healthy so that concern and worry over the future is eliminated as much as possible. Through informed planning for and consideration of future needs, we can create an environment of heightened control and mastery over the future. To be sure, no matter how carefully we plan our futures, we cannot totally eliminate the unknown, the unexpected, and the unpredictable in our lives. We need to be psychologically ready to deal with precipitous and inevitable events of life. However, knowing that such events will occur, no matter how much we've tried to prepare for every possibility, may often be preparation enough. It is the expectation or conviction that all is taken care of that sets us up most dramatically for surprise and for a feeling of being overwhelmed and betrayed by circumstance. Once again, however, our preparation for the future and the need to constantly upgrade and monitor our preparedness cannot be allowed to interfere with our ability to live now, to focus on the excitement and joy of daily living

I mentioned above that the resistance to seeking enjoyment as a primary goal in life may be related to deep-seated, psychological phenomena. There is no doubt that our comfort with seeking pleasures, or even our awareness that pleasure-seeking is a legitimate and honest pursuit for adults, is dependent upon two critical issues.

First, we learn through observation and through the modeling of behaviors and emotions we have witnessed in our parents, teachers, and other authorities who are influential in our day-to-day lives. Second, we pay special attention and ultimately internalize the specific nature of the reactions and attitudes of the surrounding world, including our parents and other authorities, to our personal expressions of euphoria, joy, exuberance, laughter, and pleasure.

When we observe our parents and significant others in our environment allowing themselves to be driven by pleasure-seeking and allowing themselves to fully experience the emotional richness of happiness, success, joy, and exhilaration, we will easily identify with the permission they give themselves to enjoy their lives. Because young children internalize in a much less discriminating fashion than do older children and adults, gross incorporations of the surrounding world's attitudes about pleasure and pleasure-seeking will be taken in. Ultimately, the children will allow themselves similar license to experience joy and gratification. And they will continue to do so into their adult years.

But if a child's models for identification are ambivalent about pleasure-seeking, or worse, reluctant to allow pleasure as a natural experience, so too will the child incorporate these attitudes and will become conflicted over the legitimacy of feeling satisfied and pursuing self-gratifying activities. And this attitude will persist, perhaps even intensify, as his life proceeds. Clearly this individual will struggle later in life with structuring his time, particularly in structuring time driven by pleasure-seeking goals. He will more likely become preoccupied with pleasure-avoiding pursuits or by obligation-driven behaviors.

The joylessness we see in others and the lack of permission we give ourselves to freely pursue pleasure in reasoned and aim-inhibited ways can destine us for lives of dreariness, sadness, frustration, and disappointment. If we have not seen it in those we admire, idealize, love, and fear, where in fact shall we learn it? And from where will we learn to give ourselves permission to pursue and legitimately enjoy pleasurable time?

As children and as adults, we pay close attention to emotional reactions that the world provides to our experiences of joy, enthusiasm, exuberance, euphoria, and laughter. In fact, we pay close attention to the reaction that the world around us makes to all of our expressions of affect, not only to positive emotional reactions. But if the world is neutral, disinterested, or even negative in responding to our excitement over life, those reactions will form the origin of our future reactions to our own pleasure. If from very early on, the idealized, admired, omnipotent, all-knowing parent does not love my loving them, or laugh when I am funny, or get excited to witness my excitement, that quality of response will be registered internally. And if that happens often enough and repeatedly, I too will become ambivalent and conflicted over my own exuberance. In fact, I may even begin to consider pleasure-seeking behavior as superfluous, silly, deleterious, frivolous, and ultimately something to be avoided. It may be okay for others, but not for me. I have other, far more important goals to address!

Aging, almost by definition, makes us more aware of the passage of time. It is not that time is going faster; it's just that it's winding down. And the subjective feeling is that I still have a lot I want to do. It may not be that there is a lot I must do but a lot I still wish to do. The management of time in later life is not about finishing up what is left undone from earlier life. It's about the structuring of time so that it is meaningful and joyous.

And the nature of the particular activities that bring us meaning and joy varies for each one of us. In structuring our time for the future, it is critical that we do what is important to us. What brings ultimate joy to your friend may be totally meaningless to you. So why pursue that?

This is the time in your life when your activities and interests do not have to be presented to anyone but yourself for review. In fact, even you do not have to approve; all you have to do is give yourself permission to try anything that interests you. Perhaps this is the greatest reward of aging. We are now free to try anything reasonable, perhaps even pushing the limits of what seemed reasonable to us at an earlier age.

On Success

Success is one of those terms that we all understand in a general way but rarely explore in a personal way. Success is a nebulous term, used frequently though perhaps rather loosely. Unfortunately, more often than not, the term success refers primarily to financial success.

When we think of Bill Gates as a successful individual, it's obvious that we are referring to his capacity to generate huge sums of money for himself and others. But when we think of Albert Einstein, for example, the meaning of success clearly changes. In this instance we interpret success in terms of fame, but fame that comes from ingenuity, scientific creativity, productivity, and intellectual status.

In the case of Winston Churchill, whom many would consider a successful man, the criteria for success again changes dramatically; we might consider Churchill's success to be based on power, charisma, foresight, and ultimate faith in himself. Success for Tom Brady would be based on his athletic prowess, stamina, motivation, courage, and limitless reliance on his physical attributes. In the case of Eleanor Roosevelt, the criteria for our understanding of success changes once again; we admire her capacity to engage others in meaningful ways, to be charismatic, to be an excellent role model for women, and to remain sensitive to the needs of the poor, needy, or helpless. Given these widely divergent examples of individuals whom we would consider successful, it is critical to acknowledge the diverse criteria we use in defining success.

Success can be further considered from two perspectives. First let's explore success from the view of the outside world looking at the designated successful one. This perspective generally does not take into consideration the internal emotional experience of the successful person. In this first case, we judge success by external and objective attributes and appearances, or at least by what we perceive from an outside appraisal of the person's life and activities. We are forced to use obvious and overt societal understandings of success, such as the acquisition of power, money, status, position, traditional fame, etc. There is also the more internal, subjective, psychological view of success, which may at times be dichotomous from the external "markers" that indicate a successful person. This internal, subjective feeling of success, while harder to see and measure objectively, is a more reliable and perhaps more meaningful type of success for an individual to achieve.

This concept is pertinent to issues associated with aging, and particularly with the goal of aging "successfully." The internally experienced type of success is what we need to pay attention to in planning and considering our own aging processes. An individual's success can be thought of as an ongoing process by which one gains access to potentialities within oneself, either recognized or unrecognized, in order to achieve realistic goals one sets for oneself. True success, and by that I mean that internal feeling of success, is directly related to your awareness of who you are, what your capacities are, and how you can effectively use those capacities to create positive outcomes, according to your own idiosyncratic design. The definition of success looked at from this perspective is therefore an ever-changing, evolving state of mind and set of feelings.

The capacity for experiencing success begins early in life and continues well into later life. Clearly our potentialities and goals change as we age and become more experienced and informed, particularly as we become more knowledgeable about ourselves and the world around us. The attributes we choose to actualize at any given point will hopefully be appropriate and manageable for the specific age at which we find ourselves. The more adaptable our skills and attributes are, and especially over time, the more likely we are to feel a consistent sense of success and well-being. As we age and begin to plan how to satisfy our inner needs in the future, it is important that we examine and re-examine who we are, what we want, and what we can realistically expect of ourselves. The ability to achieve reasonable goals at any stage in life yields a feeling of success and balanced self-esteem.

If I've had the goal of being able to run a 4-minute mile (and I vividly recall Roger Bannister doing it many years ago for the first time), then I'd better try to achieve that goal when it is still possible for my body to manage the attempt. There's a pretty small likelihood that I'll achieve that goal, no matter how hard I work at it, if I begin training at age 70. So timing is critical and needs to be realistic and consistent with what you know yourself to be capable of doing.

Now, this does not exclude attempting new activities because certain endeavors are not time-related. For example, if I always wanted to be a creative writer or a photographer or engage in some entrepreneurial activity, I can certainly attempt those endeavors at any point in my life, but they may have to wait for "later" because of time, financial, or energy restraints. So, planning for your aging process has to take into consideration longstanding (but appropriate) goals you have for yourself.

Goals and ideas that were difficult to pursue because of time contraints or other obstacles could and should re-enter your awareness later in life when they are more possible to attempt. And while success is never guaranteed in any new endeavor, the focus needs to be on the attempt itself and on the value of the attempt. Perhaps in ways quite different from our traditional work lives, the outcome of the new endeavor will be far less important than the value derived from the effort itself. The goal of a particular endeavor, even a new one, has to be directed toward feeling good and raising self-esteem, not upon achieving perfection.

Individuals who derive their feelings of self-esteem and internal balance from the process rather than the specific outcome of their activities are uniquely equipped for the aging process. They will be less focused on output and outcome and more alerted to the ongoing process of trying new activities. And they will be enhanced by their efforts, even if the outcome is negative or disappointing.

I return for a moment to the example of running the 4-minute mile. If at 60 years of age I decide, even against advice of professional trainers and running experts, that I will try to run that 4-minute mile, am I simply setting myself up for bitter disappointment? Well, not necessarily. If the goal is purely on the process of training to run that 4-minute mile and my pleasure is primarily derived from trying to get ready to run it one day, then I will not be bitterly disappointed if I run that mile in 6 minutes or even in 8 minutes. I will have given my long-time dream of running that 4-minute mile value and I will have trained regularly, running and keeping in shape, watching my diet, and indirectly working out my whole body in preparation for that 4-minute run. And I will have given myself purpose and direction in one aspect of my life that I deemed important and worthy of my full effort. Not to try to achieve the dream at all may in fact be ultimately more disappointing than trying, training, and finally running, even without achieving the 4-minute mile.

It is this kind of perspective that needs to be adopted more fully as we age, including in the area of cognitive functioning. The deterioration of our physical strength will be more obvious perhaps, but if we do not challenge and utilize our cognitive abilities (mental working out), they too can diminish, but happily not nearly as quickly or noticeably as the physical. And as we age, even for those for whom physical agility and strength have been central to their self-esteem, the physical aspects of our lives become less and less relevant in terms of our overall self-evaluation. Cognitive skills are not only lost more slowly (if at all) but in certain instances can be dramatically enriched and expanded into new areas. The aging process, and particularly how we structure our time during that process, can provide us opportunities never previously considered, especially in terms of cognitive development.

From this view, the aging process seems inviting and stimulating, and can be experienced as a reward for having survived those tough, earlier years when options and opportunities may have felt closed to us. It's fascinating and even paradoxical that the commonly held idea of opportunities being more plentiful during our youth may in fact be incorrect. All too often, because of mounting obligations to family, work, friends, and ourselves, younger people may not be able to exercise the options that are apparently so plentiful. And people who have more time and energy available, namely older people, may have more freedom to pursue their unrequited dreams without obstacles.

The task then is how to become more directly aware of those unrequited dreams that we most want to pursue and to make that pursuit when time and energy become more available. Some of our most gratifying pursuits (for example, an active physical exercise program) may already be in place and are therefore to be continued and reinforced going forward. But there will also be a wish to explore new avenues for output and stimulation, and accessing these is an interesting challenge. The process of discovering these ungratified longings involves self-exploration and reflection, and is far less difficult than one might imagine. Gaining increasing knowledge of oneself and one's hidden interests can come from within and from without.

Sources from without may include your spouse, your children, good friends, former colleagues from work or play, or from any person who knows or understands you well. It is also true that professionally trained individuals may be able to assist in this exploration, but they are not absolutely necessary for this process. Many of us remain "blinded" to our own proclivities, for a wide variety of reasons, but others who know us well may have interesting suggestions and ideas about our interests and may have gained significant clues regarding our hidden wishes. While they may be hidden to us, they may be more obvious to those who love us. Thus, open dialogue with those closest to you may yield extremely useful information.

The other source, which on the surface appears more obvious, is information about you that comes from within yourself. There are overt clues, but one has to recognize them when they appear. But how and where do I find them? We each have longstanding interests and fascinations, but we often say, "Well, I'll get to those later." It is these interests that I am most specifically talking about. But others likely exist as well. Perhaps they are less overtly known to us, but they are there to be uncovered nonetheless.

While there is no fail-safe method of determining where these fascinations are buried, you can begin by a thoughtful examination of your life. Look for themes, principally for recurrent themes that seem always to have been present, either actively or passively. These themes will most often be found in persistent areas of interest, or in areas in which you already have talent and skills, or in areas in which you have considered making attempts at exploration or even taken instruction in the past, or in reawakenings of old untapped proclivities. It is rather unusual, but not completely unheard of, that individuals will uncover interests that are totally new or never before considered.

This process of finding direction, and especially new direction, can be a time-consuming, frustrating process, but it is essential for one's future "success." In fact, one could say that at any time you find yourself in the midst of a transitional time period, you must become cognizant of the pertinent issues that change stirs in you. Transitions of all sorts involve leaving something behind (it may be positive or negative) and moving toward something new, the outcome of which is not always clear. The more aware you are of the underlying issues stirred up, the more readily you will manage the transition. There's no real mystery involved in that statement. But it's not easy to achieve unless you are willing to explore your inner self.

On Retirement

A very challenging transition in the aging process is the move toward retirement, by which I mean a change from an active full-time work life to one that is either totally non-active or part-time. It is unfortunate that the understanding of retirement is often commingled with ideas of "being put out to pasture," which implies non-productivity, the end of one's earning potential, lack of stimulation, loss of power and status, loss of self-esteem, and the beginning of the "terminal" phase of life. None of these attributes ascribed to retirement make it all that appealing. It is no wonder that we tend to look at retirement with some hesitation. Instead of seeing it as the beginning of a time for enhanced opportunities and options for ourselves, it represents the beginning of the end. Why would anyone be attracted to that concept?

And yet, particularly these days when individuals tend to live longer than their parents, more and more people will be forced to address the issue of prolonged life after work. Because of a generalized reticence to look at the issues associated with retirement, people enter the retirement phase utterly unprepared for the inevitable stresses and strains that accompany this kind of transition. And yet it is evident that the more prepared you are regarding the transitional issues associated with retirement, the more likely it is that you will negotiate that phase in a successful and gratifying manner.

Despite wishes to the contrary, many, if not most of us, will have made our work life central to our day-to-day existence. And no doubt a careful examination of a cross-section of the working population would reveal widely disparate work experiences. However, one thing will very often be true despite these differences: namely, that work is at the center of American life. Thus, to choose or to be asked to give up this core structure in one's life will obviously create significant challenges. If you consider how central work is in defining American life and how it often serves as the single most important source of power, status, self-esteem, and financial security, it is easy to understand why people feel reluctant to carefully explore the issues involved in giving up work. Why should I examine any process that will force me to lose my feelings of self-worth, my position in the world, my capacity to make money, my forum for accessing and utilizing power, and the day-to-day structure that has served me well over many years? I should enthusiastically look into that? Are you kidding?

It is unfortunate that very little has been written with respect to the psychological changes associated with this particular phase of aging. A quick literature search will reveal that most retirement planning is related to financial planning, with very little or no attention paid to the emotional aspects of retirement. I strongly believe that while financial concerns are certainly important, they are by no means the most important issue contributing to a successful adaptation to later life. In fact, the focus on financial issues may distract the future retiree from addressing far more critical items in preparation for his or her eventual retirement.

The crucial preparation for retirement is best considered in two phases: the pre-retirement and post-retirement phases. The pre-retirement phase is largely theoretical and preparatory, while the post-retirement phase is when it becomes a reality, when the anticipated relations and tensions may occur. The initial phase, which occurs prior to the actual date of transitioning into non-active work life, can be met in a creative manner if the individual is open to exploring the aspects of leaving work. The gratification one derives from work must be studied and understood in order to anticipate emotional reactions associated with leaving an active work life, most notably a sense of loss. This pre-retirement phase can also include a search for supplemental interests and activities, as well as a support system that will assist in the effective management of the stresses that can accompany retirement.

The individuals who have informed themselves about the possible range of emotional reactions will not be caught off guard or feel overwhelmed when they initially experience feelings of sadness, loss of self-esteem, loss of power, loss of position, loss of income, loss of structure, or loss of regular contact with longstanding colleagues, which will be present at the onset of retirement. And the person who has developed alternate ways of satisfying these needs in other contexts will be better prepared for handling that transition.

Unfortunately, there are no guidelines or tried-and-true formats that each of us can follow exactly. Each person's program must be individualized according to their own idiosyncratic needs and wishes. And therefore it is essential that much work be done in preparation before you find yourself in the middle of the emotional hurricane without any security or safety network.

This process of preparation may sound very difficult. How do I prepare for this potentially overwhelming change? Where do I turn for assistance and guidance? If there are no common formats for figuring out what to do, what do I do? If there is little reading material from which to obtain direction, and if financial planning isn't going to take care of the major stressors, how do I proceed?

There are a number of reasonable steps that should precede the actual termination of work far enough in advance so that all parties either directly or indirectly involved in the individual's retirement can sort through the impact of the transition. It's not as if we live in a vacuum. Your retirement will directly affect your spouse, your children, your coworkers, your extended family, your friends, and other people with whom you have regular and meaningful contact. So it behooves you to address with each of those parties, and perhaps more than once (particularly, for example, with your spouse), what they can anticipate about the imminent change in circumstance and what you are antici-pating for yourself. It is critical to have your support system in place and for each member of that support system to have addressed what it means for them to have you leave active work life. The more solid and integrated the external support system, the more effectively the transi-tion will be managed by all involved parties.

The internal support system, that is, what you have done for your-self to prepare for the eventual changes in your life, is even more critical than any external preparation. In general, many people resist exploring the emotional components of leaving one's work and the expected emo-tional reactions to that change. There is the naïve sense that if I avoid addressing the emotional aspects of this transition, then perhaps it will not affect me. Unfortunately, it is quite the opposite. The less we know and understand, the more we will suffer.

On Creativity
and Productivity

Especially in American culture, productivity is a highly valued and respected personality trait. To be motivated toward productivity and therefore to engage in productive action are goals worthy of our time and attention. The image of a productive person is one who works hard at a socially acceptable endeavor that also yields a valuable outcome. The determination of whether an activity is productive or not relies principally upon the approval of that activity, either by the producer himself, or by those for whom the product is being produced.

Productivity is very different in nature than creativity. Creativity is focused more on the *process* of producing than on the *product* that results. And while the creative process covers a wide range of activities, at its core in any application is the discovery of a new way of thinking or formulating. To be creative is to throw new light or to provide a novel interpretation or understanding. This manner of thinking about creativity can be applied to a wide range of what we commonly consider "creative work." Some creative processes are truly productive; others may not yield a tangible or quantifiable end product, yet remain helpful in clarifying the unknown.

While we all strive to some degree to be both creative and productive and to embrace both attributes as best we can, I suspect that most people would choose productivity over creativity; productivity initially seems more useful. However, to be creative is to satisfy some inner longing, some reaching for greater clarity about life's mysteries. And is the creative process of the poet different from the creative process of the plumber who devises a new method to solve a current plumbing dilemma? To the extent that creativity can be defined as the search for a new answer to a formerly unanswered question, the creative process is at least similar for the poet and the plumber.

Either activity, being creative or productive, is positive, but only when kept in balance with the rest of an individual's life experience, that is, when creativity and/or productivity do not interfere with the normal functioning of the individual. It is not uncommon to see people who are "taken over" or so obsessed by their creative or productive activity that the rest of life becomes superfluous. If creative or productive activities control life, they have passed over a critical line into deleterious functioning.

For example, an obsessed Vincent Van Gogh, perhaps driven to create art in order to answer or relieve certain internal conflicts, may indeed create works of great value, beauty, and genius, but the act of making art may yield no real emotional reward to the creator. On the other hand, if the motivation for one's art includes seeking psychological balance and artistic expression, then the art-making may serve humanity as well as the artist.

Similarly, individuals obsessed with their own productivity, those who are driven by obligation or fear to be productive, will gather precious little emotional value from their own productivity. They may obtain short-term relief from their productive work, but not enduring reward. The drive toward productivity, when in harmony with other pleasure-seeking goals in life, can be very enriching. But when that drive obliterates all else, the result is that a trait like industriousness that could have been a personality strength becomes a liability.

This phenomenon is often seen in personality functioning; that is, when a strength is overused or over-relied upon, or is driven by uncontrolled obsession and stays active irrespective of whether or not it yields pleasure to the individual. The strength then becomes a weakness or detriment to the personality. When a strength is kept in balance with the general functioning of the self, then it will consistently provide heightened self-esteem and emotional well-being.

When people find themselves with extra time on their hands, unutilized energy, or unexplored interests, a move toward creative and/or productive activity can add enormous excitement to their lives. For instance, when people who are aging can effectively locate their interests, they can indulge in creative or productive endeavors without any need for quantifiable benefit. Later in life, it's all about quality of experience and the intellectual/emotional/physical rewards derived from activity. And to the degree that we can act without concern for the value of our output, we are free to enjoy the acting itself. To be productive or creative in our activity will add a degree of reward, but the primary reward comes simply from the act itself.

For most people, especially those for whom work was highly structured, there can be great difficulty in locating areas of interest after the structured work ends or is dramatically cut back. This can be true even if their work was rich and gratifying. When older people can experience their increased freedom as reward for having successfully reached that stage of life, and not as the endpoint of productive living, then opportunity will abound for creative and productive utilization of their time.

Too many individuals consider creative activity to be solely exemplified by the creation of beautiful pieces of art or by deftly crafted prose or poetry. Creativity can be far simpler and more easily achieved than one might imagine. It is critical to remember that the goal of any new creative activity is self-enhancement and the utilization of one's skills in new ways; the value of creative undertakings is absolutely not contingent upon the aesthetic beauty created. The sculptor can find pleasure in each and every chip of marble his chisel carves out. He does not have to wait for the grand unveiling of the finished sculpture for his gratification. The same is true for the beginning poet, artist, gardener, entrepreneur, photographer, hiker, biker, etc. To be creative is to find new solutions to old questions through your unique skills and talents. In the process of seeking workable solutions and then applying them, you also rediscover your vitality and humanity.

On Youth and Youthfulness

Attitudes about youth and youthfulness dramatically impact feelings about the aging processing in ourselves and in others around us. Youth can be thought of in physical, emotional, and psychological terms, each containing diverse criteria. Youth in the physical sense of the word usually refers to the freshness, vitality, strength, beauty, and attractiveness (and thus desirability) of the body. Needless to say, this aspect of youthfulness is well understood by all of us, even though each of us may have our own definition of "young and beautiful." And the longing to maintain a youthful and attractive physical presence is reasonable and understandable.

The physical idealization of youth is placed before our eyes with incredible frequency. Advertisements, billboards, movies, newspapers, and magazines all bombard us on a regular basis with products to enhance our beauty, and beautiful young people are constantly exhibited as ideal. While there are some attempts to address the needs of an aging population in this physical dimension, they are likely to be focused on how to retain, reclaim, or manufacture anew your youthful appearance. We receive invitations to resurrect our "lost" physical beauty with a wide variety of new and fascinating medical advancements, procedures, and products. This bombardment is very difficult to escape and has a strong impact on an aging population.

The focus on physical youthfulness encourages one to do whatever possible, no matter the cost or the pain associated with the "resurrection of youth," to avoid the natural and graceful acceptance of an inevitable loss of somatic youthfulness. This is not to say that we should not do reasonable and sensible things to maintain youthfulness and physical health, such as participating in regular exercise, having a healthy diet, watching one's weight, getting adequate sleep, planning for relaxation and play times, allowing adequate time for rejuvenation of physical and emotional and psychological health, and participating in activities that maintain a youthful body.

As in so many other areas of life, we each need to discover a balanced approach in which life's foci are distributed more or less evenly among a wide range of important life goals. Unfortunately, too often people are massively overly focused on youthful appearance and resisting the physical aging process, no matter the cost. Is it really any wonder that so many people, men and women alike, become obsessively preoccupied with physical youth, given the continuous bombardment of materials that champion a youthful appearance?

However, an excessive focus on the physical aspects of aging is not simply a response to external forces. It is also related to the internal psychological reaction of each individual to the inevitable process of physical aging. Especially if physical beauty has been used to compensate for feelings of frustration and disappointment, there will be a desperate need to retain the compensatory attribute as long as possible. For some people, physical beauty and attractiveness become rationalizations for many other perceived failures and disappointments, and therefore remain the principal source of self-esteem. Sadly, even this source will eventually be lost. In this case, the idea of physical aging is simultaneously repugnant and mortifying; when inevitable physical changes do occur, a person can become overwhelmed with despair, grief, panic, and/or a sense of urgency. It's as if someone has torn away their life raft, leaving them stranded at sea. All the public focus on beauty and its infinite retention plays to this vulnerability. Thus any means whatsoever to preserve youth and youthful appearance seems worth trying and clinging to. The acceptance of aging becomes completely untenable. But at what emotional and psychological expense?

From a psychological perspective, youth and youthfulness are associated with having an infinite number of options and opportunities, with limitless hope, enthusiasm, and expectation, with boundless energy, creativity, and potential, and with seemingly infinite time to live, achieve, actualize dreams, and change course if obstacles arise. However, as I've come to understand through my own life experiences and the observation of others, the highly idealized attributes supposedly attributed to youth are largely fictional. While there may well be some individuals who pass through childhood relatively unscathed from psychological trauma, and therefore carry with them no fears or restraints on their freedom to exercise all options, such individuals are more the exception than the rule. I cannot recall meeting anyone who fully satisfies those criteria.

In truth, we all become psychologically scarred to one degree or another, and therefore have areas of restraint, fears of failure, aversion to risk, lack of discipline, or vulnerable self-esteem in certain areas. Not that we can't work on these areas of vulnerability; most of us can and do, through careful self-reflection and self-analysis, learning from the errors of our psychological and characterological patterns of behavior, and making adaptive changes in order to function more effectively. But this is neither a simple nor a short process. On occasion it may require professional intervention and assistance.

The point is that while youth is theoretically a time of limitless options, the inevitable obstacles to true feelings of success must be slowly "exorcised" and worked through in order to experience the fullness of our abilities and potentials. I feel that the envy of youth and youthful exuberance and options are overstated and wasteful of valuable energy. In fact, mature individuals who have risen above (although never completely) their idiosyncratic psychological obstacles to success and self-esteem, and who have creatively utilized their particular talents tend to have more opportunity to feel successful in their endeavors than the young and enthusiastic. Youthful years are often spent "finding oneself and one's direction," and less so in enjoying the fruits of one's successful endeavors. The mature population is more able to enjoy the fruits of successful endeavors and less likely to be consumed with finding oneself and one's direction. In fact, perhaps younger people have reason to envy the circumstances of more mature people for this reason, but that would be wasteful of energy as well.

By maturity I am referring to the sense of self that comes from having lived, examined one's experiences, and made adjustments based upon these self-examinations. Maturity entails a deep sense of knowing and understanding one's internal and external universe; it is not based on having reached any particular age. For some individuals maturity can come quite early in life, and for others, never.

In the process of emotional and psychological aging, we experience growth in our ability to analyze and neutralize negative effects from any source, and to understand the source of emotional conflicts that give rise to the particular affective experience. To truly know yourself is to recognize familiar emotional and psychological reactions, and to then know how to adapt and adjust those reactions so that they are less disruptive, less frequent, less intense, and less intrusive. This process clearly takes time and determined effort.

It is often the case that a major psychological event becomes instrumental in initiating a maturation process, even later in life. These moments may be associated with intense pain, loss, fear, etc. If not too overwhelming, such intense events can promote a process of introspection, growth, and maturity.

From a psychological standpoint, maturity represents the ability to rely on one's self and one's emotional resources to deal with whatever traumas may be presented along life's road. While no one of us ever escapes periodic bouts of stress and tension, and even moments of great trauma and disappointment, how we deal with those moments is largely dependent upon how psychologically prepared we are from having processed psychic assaults in the past. Each moment of psychological tension may have innate differences and attributes peculiar to that moment, but they will still ring familiar bells somewhere within the psychological system. And the degree to which one has reflected on the past and has access to unconscious aspects of internal reactions will dramatically impact one's ability to manage the latest assault.

Young people tend not to have this kind of resilience without adequate life experience. Thus while young people theoretically have time and energy and a wide range of opportunities available to them, because of a relative lack of life experience and the ability to accurately weigh the importance of one option over another, they might be unable to take full advantage of their options. George Bernard Shaw's quote suggesting that "youth is wasted upon the young," while smacking of some envy, also rings with truth.

How many times have you said, "I'd love to do it all again, knowing then what I know now"? But those two phenomena are mutually exclusive. Knowing what you know now only came through the experiences and self-reflection that occurred during your passage from youth into later life. Frankly, I'd rather be right here than have to repeat the turmoil of finding myself and my way in earlier years. The ultimate reward of aging is knowing, becoming wise, and understanding the ins and outs of our internal and external worlds.

RELATIONSHIPS AND AGING

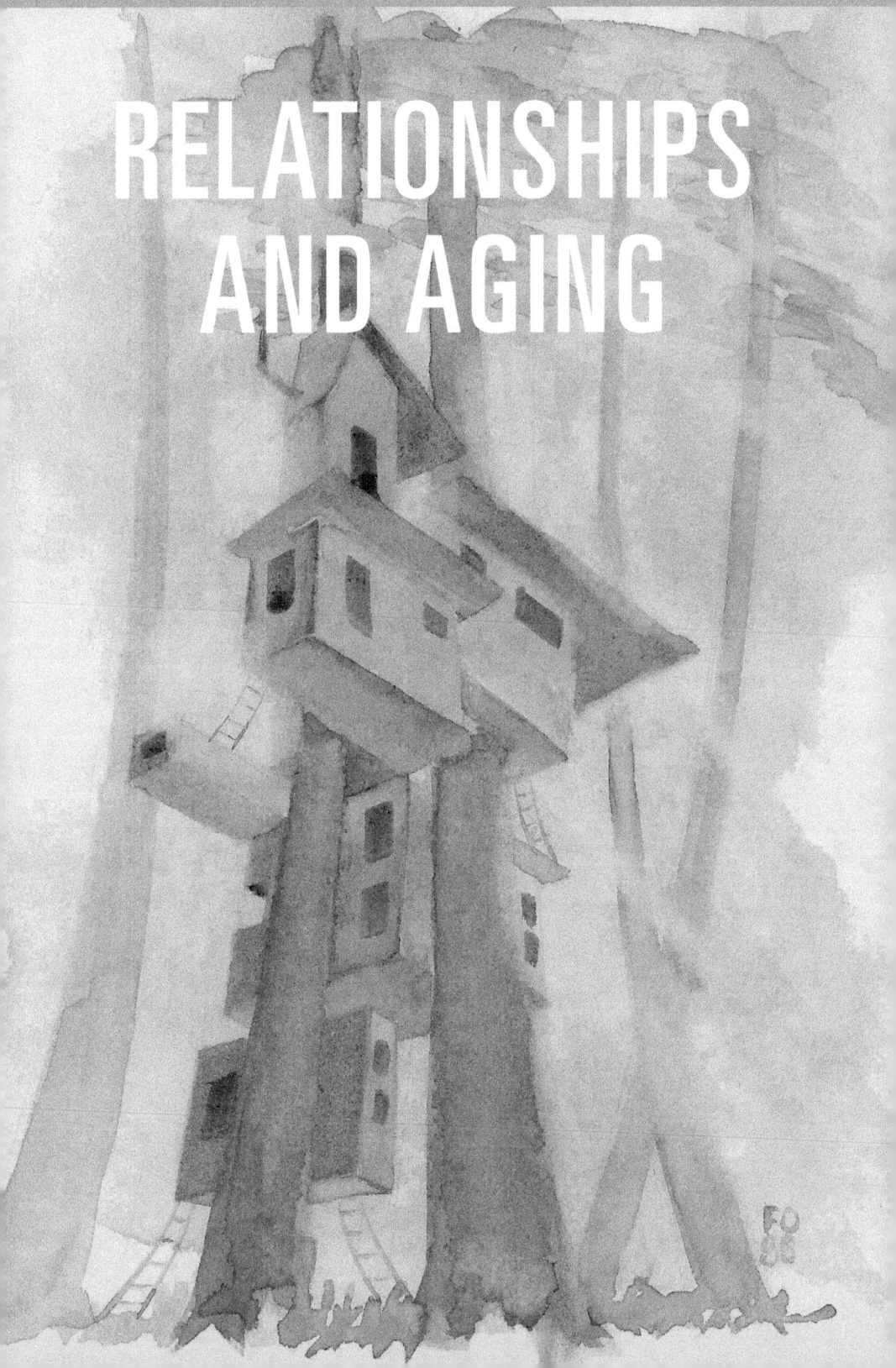

On Knowing and Being Known

Relationships with others are the epicenter of emotional life. Relationships that prove reliable over time yield a consistent, predictable flow of warmth and self-esteem for individuals. However, unreliable relationships or a general lack of interpersonal connections can create a gaping hole that becomes one's primary focus and concern. This kind of vacuum sucks energy and distracts one from other creative and valuable activities.

Relationships, and particularly those that have closeness and empathy as primary attributes, result in two important outcomes, namely "knowing the other" and "being known by the other." Neither of these experiences occurs by accident. They both require a particular kind of emotional work that includes curiosity, sensitivity, empathy, the ability to listen and communicate, and the willingness to take emotional risks. The risks that need to be taken include opening oneself up to potential exposure and criticism from others, and expressing one's opinions and perceptions without censorship or restraint.

The ability to comfortably relate to others is highly contingent upon the nature of early relationships with significant objects in one's environment. An optimal environment, one defined by closeness, understanding, and non-judgmental attitudes, will encourage a child to actively engage others. And that child will expect to find a warm and receptive world. But if early interactions are conflictual, unempathetic, critical, or isolating, that child will approach others with trepidation, mistrust, and self-protectiveness. If one's fear of closeness and intimacy becomes too pronounced, it can lead to a feeling of social isolation. This latter individual will avoid close human contact and resist being open, communicative, or engaging.

Happily, most of us fall between these two polar opposites of human interactional experience. Only rarely are childhood experiences exclusively positive. Thus, we all carry some degree of "scarring"; we have all known disappointment, frustration, and suffering in our relationships. However, for most of us, close interaction with others yields more positive feelings than negative, leaving us willing to explore connections to others and able to enjoy those connections when they occur.

A strong sense of self-esteem comes primarily from our own self-evaluations and self-approval. And the acquisition of balanced self-esteem is the goal of growth and development. To become increasingly individuated, independent, and self-sufficient, but also maintain the capacity for close interactions with others, nourishes a balanced sense of self. It is quite a different thing to want close contact because it yields pleasant and affirming feelings than to need close contact for emotional equilibrium, almost like an addiction. Thus, while the self-esteem that is derived from our own discriminating evaluation of our selves is central, self-esteem can also be derived from the discriminating approval of others. The approval of others is the "icing on the cake," but it's a cake we must bake ourselves beforehand. While we all seek approval, acceptance, affirmation, and reflection from others, they must not be the only source of our internal sense of well-being and balance.

The communication between two individuals provides some of the greatest rewards of intimacy. The sharing of ideas and the understanding of each other's positions result in the sense of knowing the other person well and being well known at the same time. And can there exist a more pleasurable feeling than the intimacy of two minds meeting, each coming away from the interaction feeling more knowledgeable and understood? This synergy can occur even without agreement on all the issues discussed. In fact, the discussion of differing viewpoints among individuals adds significantly to our knowledge base. Ideally, friendly disagreement should be welcomed, as long as the discussion is not interrupted by acrimony. Again the capacity to be open to learning is critical. A closed mind cannot ever find true closeness with another.

As we age, we carry our expectations about human interaction with us. We develop a pretty good sense of what to expect from relationships in general, and we come to understand their value and meaning. However, the free time, available energy, and heightened willingness to be experimental and exploratory that often accompany the aging process can alter one's long-held beliefs regarding human interactions. Contrary to popular belief, aging individuals can at times be available for dramatic change in their attitudes about human interaction, particularly if they form unexpected relationships that turn out to be positive.

Because we have more time available to us as we age, it behooves us to be attentive to this issue of active communication with others, beginning with those closest to us, including spouses, siblings, children and grandchildren, relatives, and friends. We must stay open to new contacts too. Through an ever-widening circle of interesting discussants, we stay stimulated and interested in learning. In terms of effective time management, close connections and communication with others can be at the very center of our personal program for aging. Individuals who have been accustomed to sharing ideas throughout their lives, without any prejudgment or intense need to be right or smarter than the other person, will be uniquely equipped for this mode of pleasure-seeking.

Through lively and open communication with others we obtain the most significant bonus of all, namely we learn and discover more about ourselves. We learn by listening carefully to the wise words of our close associates, but also by listening to ourselves and never ceasing to question, "Why did I just say that?" or "How did I come to that idea?" It is through open conversation with others and thoughtful reflection on our own conceptualizations that the expansion of our selves continually progresses without a specific goal in mind. Thus, consistent, open contact and sharing with others allow us to feel better known by others, to know others better, and ultimately to know ourselves better as well.

On Family

No matter where, when, or how we grew up, the concept of family has almost certainly loomed large in each of our minds. Family is accepted by most of us as the center of our emotional and intellectual universes. Family membership often sits at the center of our day-to-day lives as well, even later in life, but especially when we are younger. As young children, our parents, grandparents, siblings, aunts, uncles, and cousins are often the most important individuals in our lives. They provide the earliest and therefore the most influential social experiences, offering us opportunities to experience joy, togetherness, cooperation, connection, and community.

Unfortunately, interactions with family members often provide us with our earliest and most intense experiences of disappointment, anger, competition, disruption, envy, jealousy, guilt, and shame. Despite the inevitable family tensions, there is a non-specific, but tangible, palpable bond that ties one family member to the other, no matter what. Although there are certainly exceptions, the family bond most often yields immeasurable value and security to each family member.

One of the most significant functions of family is that it provides a sense of continuity and tradition, which contributes mightily to an internal feeling of belonging and stability. And even though families today are far more scattered than they once were, particularly geo-graphically, the mere knowledge that my cousin or my sister is coming to visit will bring feelings of eager anticipation and expectation. The connection and reconnection allows for a sense of continuity. What is it that allows for the instant reconnection with a family member, no mat-ter how much time and distance there is between the two of you? It is the unspoken and palpable bond that we all understand and rely upon that allows for this instant reconnection.

This feeling of instant connection and belonging is not found solely in families. For example, while traveling in a foreign country, should you happen to unexpectedly encounter another American citizen, you will likely feel an immediate tie to that person, whereas in America that same tie would never or rarely be acted upon unless you knew the person reasonably well. However, a chance meeting in a distant locale may lead you to "hook up" with a fellow countryman. The longing for familiarity and connection with others is a ubiquitous and reliable motivation for contact with others of similar faith, background, nation-ality, gender, etc.

Overtly turning to one's family members for help in times of crisis can be a very comforting choice. We tend to expect a certain response from family members, namely that they will be more or less eager to provide assistance and will not turn us away. There is a common assumption within families that we take care of our own whenever possible. To turn away from a request for help by a family member is potentially to be frowned upon or even ostracized by others within the family membership. While this dynamic is true of group psychology in general, it is most potent within closely knit families.

For an aging population, one's family and one's usual function within the family often become especially soothing. To feel that you are available to others should they need you, and that you have a fail-safe supportive network with other family members should you need it, is a great source of solace and tranquility. Therefore, it is sometimes difficult to understand why some older people feel compelled to move to warmer climates, away from family and familiarity, for extended stretches of time, or even permanently. This kind of move sometimes substitutes "quality of weather" for "quality of life," which is a rather unrewarding trade-off, especially given the increased need for family connection later in life. A permanent move later in life, unless there are truly no significant connections in your "home" environment, including children, grandchildren, siblings, significant friends, gratifying activities, and associations can be a hard concept to embrace. One trades what is familiar, predictable, and often nurturing for a chance at a new beginning. But, alas, all transitions require much energy and effort. In all cases, the prospect of moving on a permanent basis, or even for protracted time periods, needs to be carefully examined.

To a lesser extent one could even question the whole issue of traveling. Travel can certainly be stimulating, enhancing, informative, and enjoyable. But the motivation for travel needs to be explored, particularly repetitive or compulsive travel. If one travels solely to fill up time and space or to escape difficult circumstances, it can never be gratifying. There can be temporary relief but not true gratification. As Ralph Waldo Emerson states in his essay entitled "Self-Reliance": "My giant goes with me wherever I go." A change in geography can never offer more than a transient solution to bigger problems. Since you take yourself along, the problems will re-create themselves no matter where you "escape" to.

Often we hear of a recent retiree touring the world right after retirement, but before she has finished the first trip, she is already planning the next voyage and the next voyage after that. What is she avoiding? The fact of her retirement and her lack of preparation for it? Or perhaps something troubling her at a deeper level? The sooner she discovers the source of her insatiable drive for travel (in which we see and feel and taste new things), and comes to terms with the true "new" thing in her life, the happier she will eventually be.

In general, major transitions are best handled by staying in an environment of familiarity and support until the changes are more effectively managed. To run frenetically in search of external stimulation and diversion in order to quell internal emotional disruption is tantamount to a rat chasing its tail on the treadmill. Much activity is occurring but no real progress.

Because retirement provides enhanced opportunities for self-exploration and outside exploration, these opportunities should be taken full advantage of. However, travel of the "outside" type, namely geographical, cultural, or social exploration, can be done without abandonment of safe and familiar infrastructure, i.e., the infrastructure provided by the family network. As in all separations in life, and especially in separations that occur early in life, one can continually "step forward" while at the very same time keeping "half an eye" focused on the safe haven of home and family. In fact, an awareness of a safe haven to which one can return encourages wider and more adventuresome travel "outwards."

Because aging can dramatically limit one's ability to create situations "de novo," reliable family connections can become extremely valuable. Family can become the one context in which you feel reasonably assured that others want the best for you and can be recruited to help you with large, immediate, or even intangible problems. Effective family membership requires ongoing work, particularly in making yourself available to others should they need you, and in being able to take your problematic issues to appropriate family members for potential intervention. Our immediate family, where we can reasonably expect to find empathy and understanding, is one of the most reliable and predictable sources of positive reinforcement available to all of us.

The sense of belonging to a greater group, particularly a cohesive, well-functioning family group, enhances a feeling of security, self-esteem, and personal empowerment. Families tend to have unique and idiosyncratic rules and regulations for belonging, and those members who follow the "rules" most closely will be drawn closer to the center of the family. They will be readily invited into "action central," the source of decision-making and power within a family.

Unlike larger group functioning, the psychology of family groups provides established members with greater latitude and acceptance should behaviors fall outside of regularly accepted patterns. Sure, there may be harsh criticism for behaviors "outside of the box," but even extremely offensive behaviors will most often be effectively managed before the member is summarily dismissed from the family structure. In other words, conforming to accepted family group behaviors will more or less secure your position within that group indefinitely, and divergent behaviors are more likely to be worked with and constructively supported over a longer time period than in non-family groups.

Not only does family provide the safe haven function, it also provides us with an opportunity to contribute to our family members, to introduce ideas, resource, direction, information, and understandings gained through our own life experiences. We are given the unique opportunity to contribute support as well as to receive it. And we can feel significantly enhanced in our self-esteem by making useful and positive "gifts" to the well-being of younger family members and to our aging contemporaries.

In this way, families offer unique opportunities to create legacy, probably better than most settings. By legacy I mean that which is left behind after we are no longer "on the scene." The greater our contributions to the well-being of our family members, the greater the legacy we leave behind. Most people are not motivated to create legacy for self-aggrandizement but rather as part of the transformation from personal narcissism to cosmic narcissism. In that transformation we become increasingly enriched and satisfied by that which we can do to help others, and less by enhancing our personal reputation or grandeur. One could even say that the more successful the narcissistic transformation has been, the less recognition will be required. Perhaps giving anonymously suggests the most effective transformation of all. But this is quite different than the anonymity that comes from contributing or providing nothing or through staying addicted to personal narcissism.

Individuals who remain tied to their own narcissistic aggrandizement may create statues to their greatness. But who will look at the statues, and who will care to remember their acts of greatness? Legacy comes primarily through acts of true generosity, not through consciously determined efforts aimed at attaining immortality. Acts of true generosity will have long-lasting effects and are far more likely to be fondly and respectfully remembered.

Because creating legacy necessitates meaningful interaction with others, it becomes a very useful manner of managing time. And where the interactions are truly meaningful, both parties will be significantly enhanced as a result of these interactions. The older person is contributing and feels valued and respected, while the other may well feel enriched and empowered by gathering deeper and wider understandings of his universe.

Even if the younger person does not specifically remember where he gained a new understanding, the individual who helped him will still have made a significant contribution. It is never necessary for the acknowledgment to occur directly. In fact, a successful transformation to cosmic narcissism requires no acknowledgment whatsoever. The knowledge that you have contributed in some unknown way to the long-term benefit of those important to you or to the world in general can be gratification enough.

On Peace in
the Valley

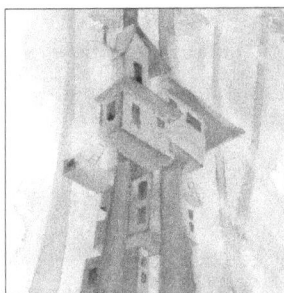

Consider the following adage: the hater suffers far more than the hated. Said another way, the person who harbors animosity toward another expends far more energy containing his animosity than does the object of the animosity, particularly if the object does not even know the quality and quantity of depressed rage directed at her. If the object of the rage discovers the angry attitude in the bearer, she might feel wounded and out of sorts, but she will not be significantly disabled by these feelings unless they evoke equal and counter-directed rage. In contrast, the hater, at times when he is consumed with animosity, will take himself right out of the game of life.

The more protracted and entrenched the animosity (whether justified or unjustified), the more negative the impact on the bearer's life. The bearer of longstanding grudges or unresolved anger reveals a narcissistic vulnerability in his behavior; the intensity of the rage is always proportionate to the intensity of pain, loss, and hurt that the bearer suffers. The rage is simply the uppermost layer of deeper pain, more easily identified and dealt with than the experience of the painful feelings themselves.

Who among us, no matter how evolved and narcissistically transformed we may be, does not have old, unresolved relationships that have fallen into disrepair but are still hidden in the deep recesses of the mind? And who among us does not have some family member who has been estranged from the central group for so long that we cannot even recall why that individual was "excommunicated" in the first place? In fact, the exclusionary act may have preceded us by decades, yet that person is still kept at bay. He or she is never included in family gatherings, and information about his or her well-being is not discussed when the family gets together.

Unresolved circumstances of any kind deprive us of critical energy that could be creatively and constructively utilized in pleasure-seeking, but instead is diverted into "standing watch" over old conflicts. Despite the effectiveness of the repression or suppression of conflictual relationships, these coping mechanisms remain economically unsound. We pay with energy we are not even consciously aware of expending.

Thus, for two very important reasons we must periodically search our histories, seeking out relationships or situations that remain on shaky ground. To the extent that we can rectify whatever wrongs were done in the past (in either direction), and can find and establish a higher ground and a more stable foundation for that relationship, the more we will be at peace with ourselves. On the one hand, we will have shown generosity to the other half of the problematic relationship and brought some modicum of peace back to the valley. On the other hand, we will have liberated our own energy from standing guard over the unresolved conflicts, bringing it back to the front lines to engage in creative and pleasurable activity. All parties come out ahead in such a resolution.

Sigmund Freud had a wonderful analogy regarding the effective utilization of psychic energy. He said that we have a certain amount of psychic energy available to us every day, and it is like an army with a certain number of soldiers available for battle. He stated that each unresolved conflict that exists unconsciously in our minds, is like a fortress that requires a number of soldiers to guard the fortress, making the soldiers at the front lines actively fighting the battles of every day fewer in number. Thus, when we deal with and resolve conflict, those soldiers that have been utilized in guarding those fortresses, and thus hanging back to do so, can then be on the front lines, to tackle problems and create anew, thus adding strength to the army's offensive and defensive positions.

To the extent that we can "clean up" our messes, and especially with individuals most important to us, we will have unburdened ourselves of unconscious, unnecessary, and costly psychological weight. If the goal of aging is to be as free as possible for the pursuit of reasonable and pleasurable activities for ourselves, then the less burden weighing us down and draining our energy the better.

It is also a source of significant self-esteem to "make right" what may have been "wrong" for a period of time. It takes energy, stamina, and strength of personality to tackle these difficult issues, but the results are well worth the effort. Even failed attempts at resolution can be self-esteem building. We can still be proud of our efforts at compromise and resolution even in a situation of deep, longstanding acrimony. Despite failure we can feel free of the guilt and shame that arise from not attempting a resolution at all. Obviously it is necessary for both parties in a conflict to be open to resolution. We only need to feel responsible for our part in a failed attempt.

Estranged family members, as mentioned above, deserve special attention. Because you may not have been directly involved in the initial exclusionary actions, you may be more able to attempt compromise and to reverse the estrangement. But if you have been more directly involved in the estrangement, then you will likely have energy tied up in keeping that person at a distance, which is a waste of useful energy. In this case you have even more reason to attempt resolution of that relationship. And who knows what gifts that estranged person may bring to the family mix? It nurtures all individuals involved, and the family in general, to resolve hidden and energy-consuming conflict among family members.

While we may not resolve every piece of unfinished business in our psychology reservoir, the more resolution we can achieve, the greater our personal reward. And if aging is about taking on challenges that we may not have previously recognized or made time for, what better challenge than trying to resolve old friendships and situations that have gone awry for any number of reasons. It is important to remember that the goal of peace-making is not to be loved by all, but to be more self-respecting. To create "peace in the valley" whenever you can is also to bring contentment to yourself.

On Sexuality

If you buy into the surface hype around sexuality and accept all aspects of its alleged impact on American life, then you could be led to believe that it's the only show in town. When was the last time you saw a commercial on television marketing a car or clothes or vacation destination or exercise facility that did not include some direct or indirect suggestion of sexual activity? So much of what we see at the movies, in the media, or on billboards alludes often and explicitly to sexuality.

We are besieged with a flood of superfluous, superficial imagery, creating the sense that sexuality and sexual behaviors preoccupy our minds much of the day. And if they don't, what's the matter with you? No doubt there are individuals who are obsessed with sexual matters, but for most of us, while it does have an important and at times prominent place, sex is not the be-all and end-all of living. To be sure, as young adolescents its place in our mind can supervene and crowd out any other issue, but even at that stage of life, it does not consume every waking minute. And to think otherwise is to buy into the marketing hype we are exposed to on a consistent basis.

Sexuality can be driven by many different motives. It may be the mutual, shared experience of a mature love relationship. It may be a forum for the expression of dominance and power of one person over another. It may be a stage for the expression of the most masochistic and self-punitive drives in a person's life. It may be an ongoing source of income for those willing to sell their sexuality to others. It may be the process by which early bodily exploration and mutual physical curiosity get expressed without any sexual goals. It may be the forum for perverse and deviant psychological expression. It may be a vehicle for titillation and temptation, without any intent for the consummation of sexual acts. It may be the mode of manipulative control of one person over another.

Additionally, sexual behaviors and sexuality may have absolutely nothing to do with sexual motives whatsoever. Sex can be the expression of subdued or overt violence perpetrated by one person on another. Sexual behaviors can also be purely about the expression of personal narcissism. An example of this motive might be: "Look at me, aren't I beautiful and desirable?" Or it can even be: "Look at us, aren't we beautiful and desirable?" Neither the narcissistic motives nor the violent motives have much to do with true sexuality. Of course, the list of possible motives for sexuality and sexual behaviors of all types is virtually endless.

Because of this multitude of motives for people's interest in sexual matters, it is hard to get a true read on the relative preoccupation we allegedly have with sexuality. Clearly there are people who reveal addictive qualities in managing their sexual behaviors, but for the overwhelming proportion of people, sexual behaviors and interests are fairly pedestrian. Most sexual behavior is motivated by a wish for closeness and intimate connection between partners. And physical connection is an effective means for the expression and deepening of an already existent emotional connection. This most typical drive for sexual union with one's partner mentioned above, while lacking some of the drama we are encouraged to believe is truly at the source of most sexual behaviors, is a healthy, balanced, reasonable goal shared between two people.

Perhaps some of the mystique associated with sex is that in many environments, particularly during our formative years, sex carries a

distinctive taboo. This taboo can stifle normal curiosity and exploration of sexual matters at more appropriate times later on, particularly
if the taboo has been formulated in a harsh and unyielding manner.
And so the pursuit of sexuality and sexual behaviors takes on hidden
and forbidden qualities instead of being seen as a wholesome, natural
part of growing up. To the extent that people see sex as forbidden, or
even evil, there will be unnecessary and often guilt-inducing qualities
added to the mix. Any specific inhibitions in this area can diminish
one's capacity for joy, adventure, experimentation, and general ease
with sexual matters.

Like so many other issues, attitudes about sexuality often come
from significant authority figures, usually fairly early in our lives. The
liberal, informed, non-judgmental, engaging parental figure, who is
open to his or her own sexuality, will create an environment conducive
to the development of healthy and balanced attitudes toward sexuality
in their children. Needless to say, the reverse is also true. That is, the
degree of inhibition in parents or parenting objects in a child's environment will be reflected in the child's struggle with the development
of healthy attitudes and behaviors in the sexual arena. More than in
most areas of emotional development, the attitudes regarding sexual
behavior in authority figures around the young child will leave a major
imprint on the child.

It is often the case, fortunately, that as people age, despite bodily
changes that one would think might inhibit sexual behaviors, mutually
satisfying sexual behavior continues with gusto, enthusiasm, and joy.
While the frequency of sexual contact between longstanding partners
may diminish over time, the capacity for joy and pleasure when they do
indulge will be there as potently as it was many years earlier.

Despite the "disgust" that younger adults may experience when
imagining their parents, or older people in general, having sexual contact, that sexuality does occur nonetheless and with more exuberance
and excitement than younger adults might expect. Like so many other
activities that require time, relaxation, togetherness, and patience,
older adults generally have all of these attributes at their disposal, so

sexual activity can be rewarding. And like many other areas of value, it is not the quantity of an action but the quality that brings the most happiness and satisfaction. This is certainly true with sexual activity in later life.

What exactly is sexual arousal? It is both a physiological and psychological response in unconscious libidinal urges. The question becomes, where does the arousal originate? Is it simply that even without any external stimulation, and with a certain frequency and predictability perhaps different for each of us, we become aware of mounting urges within ourselves that require discharge? This suggests a kind of hydraulic model of sexual drive. When enough tension is built up, then we seek discharge. This concept has some appeal in certain circles, suggesting, for example, that men must periodically discharge their precious semen somewhere, the site of this discharge being irrelevant.

The problem with this very simplistic model of sexuality is that it neglects the psychological aspects. If you accept this concept, then all sexuality becomes strictly a "build up-discharge" model of sexual interest and activity. This is not a very romantic or exclusive experience and has a more animalistic nature to it. And yet under the right set of psychological circumstances, namely, where sexual contact is more about the expression of power, control, or conquest, or even about hostile aggression directed at another, sexuality may in fact have this non-specific, non-discriminating object quality to it.

The psychological component of arousal is primarily responsive to the presence of fantasy, both conscious and unconscious fantasy. Whether arousal begins from an external source or an internal source, it stimulates fantasy formation of sexual activity. When we find ourselves with a person close to our idealized version of a sexual partner, we are easily brought to a state of arousal. However, this also requires a fantasy of one's self that is appealing and self-esteem enhancing. In other words, it is not enough to find yourself with an attractive or appealing partner based on a wide variety of factors that qualify the individual as being attractive (not just physical attributes), it must be that you see yourself as worthy, attractive, and appealing as well. The closer the perceived reality is to our unconscious fantasies of "attractive and arousing," the more intense the psychologically based sexual response. Barring any physiological obstacles, psychological arousal will evoke a state of arousal on a physical level as well.

But the psychological components of sexuality are fraught with potential difficulties. Once again, experiences and attitudes about sexual contact, carried more or less actively in our minds, will dramatically imprint upon sexual performance, enjoyment, and openness. Feelings of self-esteem and balanced narcissism may well be the major determining factor in successful sexual experience. The motives for sexual union in either partner will ultimately affect the outcome.

All too often we are utterly unaware of unconscious motives, attitudes, and feelings we carry regarding sexual behaviors. As in so many other arenas of life, extreme behavior is always suspect and suggestive of questionable motives. It is not any different with sexual behavior; the sexual arena offers plentiful opportunities for acting out neurotically driven and "off center" ideas and fantasies. Despite one's ability to find willing partners in extreme sexual behaviors, the ultimate psychological "yield" from each behavior could be deleterious to both partners.

It has often been said that the frequency of sexual activity between two partners is like a barometer for the relationship itself. The more connected and open they feel with one another and the more there exists an empathic understanding of one another's emotional states, the more likely there will be increased and gratifying sexual activity. This, of course, is also dependent upon physiological obstacles to sexual arousal. But where the physiological function is intact, emotional intimacy will inevitably produce physical intimacy as well.

If we had only been in touch with a fuller appreciation of this fact during adolescence, namely, that emotional and psychological harmony leads to heightened physical intimacy, life could have been so much less stressful. What we thought was so difficult to achieve, namely sexual union, albeit phase-appropriate sexual union, would have been so much less charged, conflicted, and controversial.

A discussion of sexuality also brings up the issue of attractiveness. It is very interesting how as young adolescents we think of potential sexual partners primarily from the perspective of attractiveness. As if physical attractiveness and gratifying sexual activity go hand-in-hand. Nothing could be further from the truth. While it is true that seeing raw physical beauty in a potential partner may well stimulate interest in sexual behavior, it bears little or no relationship to the eventual satisfying nature of the sexual activity itself. Satisfying sexual behavior is primarily a psychological issue. The more open to sexual behavior one is, irrespective of particular physical attributes of one or the other of the partners, the more gratifying the sexual contact is likely to be.

There are many individuals who remain inexorably bound to the concept of successful sexual activity being tied to physical beauty. And there is no way to deny that if one searches long and persistently enough, one may in fact find the longed-for combination of features in a partner. However, the obsessive search for beauty may have more to do with wounded narcissism and self-esteem than it does with finding an ideal sexual partner. In our society, the man with a beautiful woman on his arm may feel that his total self-worth has been raised a few notches. He must be quite a "man" if he can capture such an attractive trophy! But the trophy is made of "fool's gold." The shiny, new woman may not necessarily bring sexual joy or joy of any kind. While she may be delightful to look at, she may not be so delightful. As George Wither stated in a poem, "If she be not so to me, What care I how fair she be?"

The allure of "fairness" may be a trap we are subject to at one time or another in our lives. And this is not restricted to men alone, although men seem to receive the worst rap in this area. This is not restricted exclusively to young people either. We are all exposed to exhaustive advertising that suggests that who we are is largely dependent upon how we carry ourselves and whom we can attract. Who we are is also dependent on how attractive we appear and how attractive our sexual partners appear. As if successful connection is based on superficial appeal. And yet we are actively programmed to believe so.

True connection is based on compatibility in many areas of functioning, one of which is physical compatibility, but it is not the exclusive criterion for successful relationships with others. In fact, as I said before, attractiveness can be "fool's gold." What initially appears shiny may well grow dull too soon. But what is shiny (and substantive) beneath the surface can hold your interest far longer than surface glitter. It is the balance of talents and interests and activities that creates the most attractive individuals. And to be lured by one very shiny talent or interest is to court trouble along the way. It has been repeatedly stated that empty people seek out and find other empty people, and in their interaction both leave feeling emptier; full people seek out and find other full people, and in their interaction both leave feeling fuller.

Aging individuals, if they are not self-reflective, may inadvertently adopt attitudes common in society regarding the sexual activity of older people. As I said earlier, young people can feel "turned off" by the idea of older people engaging in sexual play. As a young psychiatrist in training, I had a very poignant experience with an older supervising psychiatrist. When I reported to him my feelings of shock after hearing about the robust sexual fantasies of a patient of mine, whom I did not consider very attractive or sensual, the supervising psychiatrist said, "Sex does not occur solely between the beautiful, sexy fashion model and the muscular macho, tight end for the Chicago Bears. It's everywhere, and everybody is entitled to the most erotic and sexiest fantasies." And of course he was totally correct, but at that young age I too thought that older, unattractive, non-sensual, overweight individuals wouldn't be interested in sexual matters, or if they were, they ought not be. I have never forgotten the supervisor's statement. But I'm sure I was not alone in that gross misperception back then, and I now know how commonly held that idea is in the mind of the general public.

The tragedy would be if older people also believed those misperceptions. They would be cutting themselves off from a natural, healthy part of human experience. Interest in human sexuality does not diminish with age, nor does the instinctive libidinal drive toward sexual union. But depending on our comfort levels in acting on those instincts, we will more or less make use of these interests and drives. And each gender is equally driven to seek sexual satisfaction. Contrary to the commonly held idea that men are more intense in their sexual needs, it is an equally prominent issue for women.

Successful climax to sexual activity for each partner is based far more on fantasy and feeling than on friction. And contrary to popular belief, particularly in the minds of younger individuals, "successful" sexual performance is far more dependent on shared feelings and fantasies than on style, length of time of lovemaking, or acrobatics. I believe that aging individuals have a better vantage point from which to understand that dynamic; over the years they have learned through broad experiences that what we believed to be unquestionable truth as younger children and even as young adults often turns out to be far from the truth.

In relationships where there is mutuality in many areas of the couple's functioning and where discussion is open about any and all issues, sexuality will be more frequent, pleasurable, and mutual as well. If we believe that humans are driven by a very strong impulse to emotionally connect to others, from which we derive great joy and completeness, we must also believe that humans seek strong and pleasurable physical connection with appropriate partners. To willingly cut oneself off from sexual activity in later life is to unnecessarily eliminate a healthy, robust aspect of human life.

As with other areas of our lives, aging provides us with unique opportunities to be experimental and adventuresome in the sexual area as well. By this stage of the game we can drop our age-old taboos about sexuality; we can be more curious and exploratory, especially if our partners are like-minded. It is not likely that you will dramatically change techniques and styles of sexual behavior that have been satisfying in the past, but to be open to new experience is the reward of aging. Why not in this area as well?

On Marriage

Perhaps one of the most critical factors in successfully negotiating the hurdles associated with aging is a reliable, predictable, and balanced marital relationship. While a marriage is often the primary relationship we turn to for intimacy, trust, communication, and support, it is nonetheless a hard relationship to get right. It is fascinating to consider how differently we often feel later in life regarding certain choices we made much earlier in life. For example, the criteria we considered in choosing a college to attend, a profession to pursue, a mate to commit to, or a location to work and live all undergo dramatic transformations as we mature and come to understand more fully what is meaningful and successful in any of these areas. Had we been told by idealized friends or relatives what was important in choosing a mate, how to manage a marital relationship, and what works and doesn't, and even if we would have listened carefully, most likely we would not have accepted or followed their counsel anyway. Marriage is just one of those things you have to experience firsthand in order to fully comprehend its complexities.

We come into relationships of all kinds, but especially into marital relationships, with preconceived notions and fantasies about what they can, should, and will be. But these notions are based largely upon what we have dreamed up and what we have observed directly in people around us. Our parents' marriage and the marriages of relatives or friends very close to us often form the origin of what we expect for ourselves. What we have been taught and have experienced directly about these relationships will have long-lasting and powerful images for our own futures.

If I could relate one of the most common misconceptions that leads to marital discord, even to marital disruption, I would say it is adhering to the unrealistic expectations one partner has of the other about making his or her world complete. The inevitable frustration that comes from this grand misconception can feed unconscious and at times irreparable resentment and disappointment in both partners. Only with age, experience, and honest self-reflection can we come to understand that while our partner can fulfill certain of our desires and needs, he or she cannot be expected to do it all. One's ability to know this about yourself and your partner can heal huge and divisive rents in any relationship.

As a relationship matures, particularly a marital relationship with its many shared joys and unavoidably frustrating events, the ups and downs of the couple become more integrated; such a connection will be able to provide a comfortable foundation for both individuals. As the unrealistic expectations of both partners melt away, what ideally remains is a flexible, resilient, accepting understanding of one another from which the potentially larger stresses of life (aging, illness, death) can be more effectively managed. The intimate knowing of each other and the recognition of each other's idiosyncratic strengths and weaknesses evolve over time.

It is not that all fantasies and hopes have to be eradicated in a relationship to make it truly work; only the unrealistic fantasies and dreams have to be modified and understood. Longstanding relationships of all kinds are based on fantasies that evolve over time, but chronic, unfulfilled, unrealistic wishes and dreams feed a cycle of resentment and disappointment. Examples of healthy, "evolving" fantasies include a sense of shared tradition, a history of experience over time yielding a sense of a knowable and somewhat predictable future, the joys of shared pride in children and grandchildren, later-life feelings of success and achievement, and feelings of personal empowerment and self-esteem from the experience of the relationship itself on a day-to-day basis. While these evolving fantasies may not resemble the dramatic, wildly creative fantasies of our earlier lives, they are by no means boring, mundane, unimportant, or unpleasurable. Quite to the contrary! These fantasies and eventual realities contribute heartily to the maintenance of self-esteem, emotional well-being, and to ongoing hope and pleasure in the future, whatever it may bring.

While the primary goals of any marriage are to know, support, and care for one another over time, the ability of the relationship to deal with inevitable stresses and tensions of life lies at the very epicenter of comfortable and pleasurable living for both partners. This ability to deal with stress together leads to feelings of security, reliability, and flexibility. To know for certain that "you are not alone" is to have a peaceful core feeling. And this feeling can only come with time, experience, and understanding of one's self and one's partner.

My sense is that the "bad rap" marriage often receives and the devastatingly high percentage of disrupted marriages are derived from a lack of understanding of one's self and one's partner, more specifically, of unfulfilled fantasies about the relationship. Not only do unfulfilled and unrealistic fantasies for the marriage itself get acted out in marital relationships; unfulfilled expectations and disappointments in other, non-marital aspects of life can also be carried or projected into the marital relationship. Because it is usually the most intimate and most exposed relationship we are involved with, marriage can carry the burden of all the disappointments and unrealized dreams of both partners. This can become a very heavy burden. Therefore, the marital relationship, more than any other relationship in our lives, needs to be a haven for resilience, safety, and compassionate understanding.

Because life, particularly as we age, can be fraught with change, stress, unforeseen illness, and unplanned "bumps in the road," the comfort of a resilient, reliable relationship is invaluable. And to the degree that the resilience is based on equal participation in creating and keeping a balance, the relationship will be more responsive to stress experienced by either partner.

The ability to share power in the relationship and to give up the need for control or disproportionate power contributes to the flexibility and adaptive capacities of any relationship. What we have either experienced or observed in others will determine the willingness we have to actively help our partner at times of stress or change. While everyone will openly profess a wish to be helpful to his or her mate, many of us will be psychologically and emotionally unprepared for that challenge. The greatest inhibitions to empathy for one's partner are unresolved resentment and disappointment that still exist in us and unconsciously influence our responses.

The more unresolved narcissism that remains in the individual, the more difficult it will be to share control and power and to comfortably ask for help. Un-neutralized narcissism may at times even reduce one's ability to give help, especially if there is no direct or immediate reward for one's contributions. Thus, anger and untransformed narcissism stand in the way of a reliable, supportive, and nurturing marital relationship.

If a relationship nourishes autonomy and provides a consistent, supportive "home base," both partners can effectively attempt and actualize their deeply held dreams and ambitions for themselves. A supportive and loving relationship will facilitate autonomous behavior; a diversity of interests can enhance closeness and enrich compatibility, rather than threatening the stability of the relationship.

The closest relationships do not necessitate constant contact and reassurance; the stability simply becomes a basic, understood component of the relationship. In fact, the greatest test of the flexibility and love in a relationship is whether or not both partners are able to facilitate, encourage, and protect the independence and autonomy of the other.

Rainer Maria Rilke, a famous German poet and author, wrote in his book entitled *Letters to a Young Poet*, about the possible positive or negative effect of romantic love on couples. He stated that the ultimate test of one lover's love for the other, is above all else to protect and support the autonomous and independent activity of the other. A love that stultifies creativity and independence of thought and activity is a deleterious and harmful love, and to be avoided at all costs.

A mature marital relationship, one that has survived and grown from the effective management of life's inevitable stresses, is able to deal with major crises for either partner. While a marriage cannot directly diminish the severity or gravity of a major physical or emotional assault on either partner, it can be very effective in providing support through the difficult times. The sense of having a partner through stresses of all kinds is an enormous comfort and source of security. To the extent that one feels alone in a crisis, one will hold back and become more risk-averse in one's behavior, thereby delimiting the full potentiality of pleasure-seeking activities. To be relatively alone during a crisis requires a lot of energy be devoted to "watching one's own back." A reliable partner can alleviate this needless loss of energy that could be put to more healing or more pleasurable use.

The care and feeding of a marital relationship goes on endlessly, even for very positive and mature relationships. Chronic neglect, lack of gratitude for loving acts, or disinterest for any reason can sow the seeds of resentment and disruption in even the best relationships. Attention must always be paid to nurture and care for what may be the single most important and comforting component of the aging process. To not do so, for any reason, is to court potential disaster, particularly at a time when the need for supportive and reliable contact grows daily.

While none of us will ever achieve perfection as an effective, loving, and endlessly patient mate for our partners, it behooves each and every one of us to keep our "eyes on the ball" and to not slip into a state of disinterest, discontent, or lack of true appreciation for the contributions of our partner. Your very future is dependent upon the health of this connection.

On Grandparenting

Nobody could ever have prepared me for this experience. I certainly felt the same lack of preparedness when I first became a parent. I've always felt that being a parent was the most exciting, most gratifying, most anxiety-producing, most frustrating, and most growth-enhancing activity I have ever taken on. Parenting gave me, and even now gives me, the greatest sense of pride I've ever known. This is a pride both in the children I helped to raise, and in myself for the consistent, persistent, encouraging, and patient attitudes I tried to embrace as a parent.

The pleasure of being a parent came in the day-to-day time with my children, encouraging, praising, directing, comforting, limiting, and loving them. And long before the outcome of their upbringing could be realistically evaluated, if one would ever really do that, I felt proud of them for their efforts and stamina, and proud of myself for my efforts and stamina through the whole process. And that process continues even with adult children, long after I thought it would. Not that there haven't been disappointments along the way, but they pale hugely in comparison with the joy. Most of the difficult, frustrating moments of raising children have by this point been woven into the fabric of my life and the specifics of the frustrations blurred by time.

Could there be anything more gratifying than adult conversations with your own children? They are people whom you know very well, perhaps better than most, and who presumably know you very well too. The interchange that derives from this knowing of one another facilitates a depth and breadth of understanding and an experience of boundless empathy and intuition. These exchanges with my children are among the most gratifying and momentous occasions of my life.

And then along came my grandchildren with whom my role is less clear and more diffuse. I certainly have less responsibility and obligation for their day-to-day well-being than I did with my children. But who could have ever imagined the Super Glue effect many of us experience in dealing with grandchildren? I use the image of Super Glue because the attachment, concern, and preoccupation subjectively feels in some ways more intense than it ever did with my children. When I try to recall the more distant past and my feelings of connection to my children, it is hard to conjure up memories of that Super Glue feeling, although I suspect it was present in some form.

Sure, as parents, we were younger and busier and more concerned with the day-to-day stuff of life, but I believe there's something more that accounts for the subjective differences we experience with our grandchildren compared to our children. It's certainly not that we love or value the grandchildren more than we did their parents (our children), or that they need us more than their parents ever did. In fact, I don't think it's about them and their needs or about any particular set of character traits that the grandchildren bring to the table. It's about us! We're different now than we were thirty years ago. We've changed. Our attitudes about what's important in life have shifted focus. And so the grandchildren get a different us with whom to interact. I think grandchildren experience a more patient, more well-rounded, less demanding, less expectant, more approving version of us than our children did.

It is certainly true that we are less preoccupied with competing issues and activities than we were earlier in our lives, but I think that the critical difference is the issue of how we now manage our time. As I've said before, time becomes even more valuable to us as we age. We modulate and monitor our usage of time in very different ways than we did when our children were young. And despite our obvious knowledge to the contrary, experientially we thought then that time was infinite. And because it felt infinite, we attended to its passage less acutely.

Within this growing appreciation for the beauty and transience of time lies the explanation for the intense joys of grandparenting. Essentially, we are more geared toward an existential perspective with respect to time and its management. It's more about experiencing the "now" than it ever was in the past. We watch our time to be sure that we seek and find nourishment from each possible moment. I do not mean to imply that we become so obsessive about the measuring of time that we cannot make use of it. Rather, due to our more enlightened appreciation for the passage of time, pleasure-seeking becomes more primary.

As a result, our moment-to-moment interchange with our grandchildren become even more critical. We watch more, we give more, we expect less, we are more generous with our individualized attention and interest, and therefore we enjoy far more. I do not consider this fairly typical hyper-awareness of time with the grandchildren to be an overindulgent preoccupation, although I have seen that phenomenon in certain instances.

Oddly enough, behavior that our children presented with at much earlier times in their lives, which included close interactions with an "us" that was very different than the "us" our grandchildren encounter currently, may have pleased us far less than the exact same behavior from our grandchildren evokes in us now. Again, the major difference is that we now take the time to notice, savor, praise, and appreciate interactions in ways that we were not able to do with our children.

There are other explanations for the grandparent's increased attention aimed at grandchildren and for the increased pleasure derived from interactions with them. These include issues of legacy and the transformation of personal narcissism into a cosmic narcissism, all of which contribute to the increased centrality of grandchildren in the minds of aging grandparents.

The eventual transformation of individual narcissism, which has "me" at the epicenter of the universe, into a more balanced view of the world at the epicenter of life (cosmic narcissism) is a desirable and powerful transition. As this process takes hold in the individual, grandchildren become more imbued with power and value. The power that was almost exclusively associated with the self system is now transferred to the outside world. As the "me" loses its centrality in my own mind, it is replaced by that which will follow me. Thus, we see the significance associated with grandchildren.

This transition toward cosmic narcissism is not so much motivated by a wish to preserve our own importance through identification with our now powerful grandchildren, but is more motivated by a wish to "pass along the torch" to those who will come after us, to give them a sense of control over their universe and a fuller understanding of their surroundings. Said another way, we endow the world around us with the power we once utilized to enhance our personal existences. We connect ourselves to the future through this transfer of power to those who will follow.

LIVING AND LETTING GO

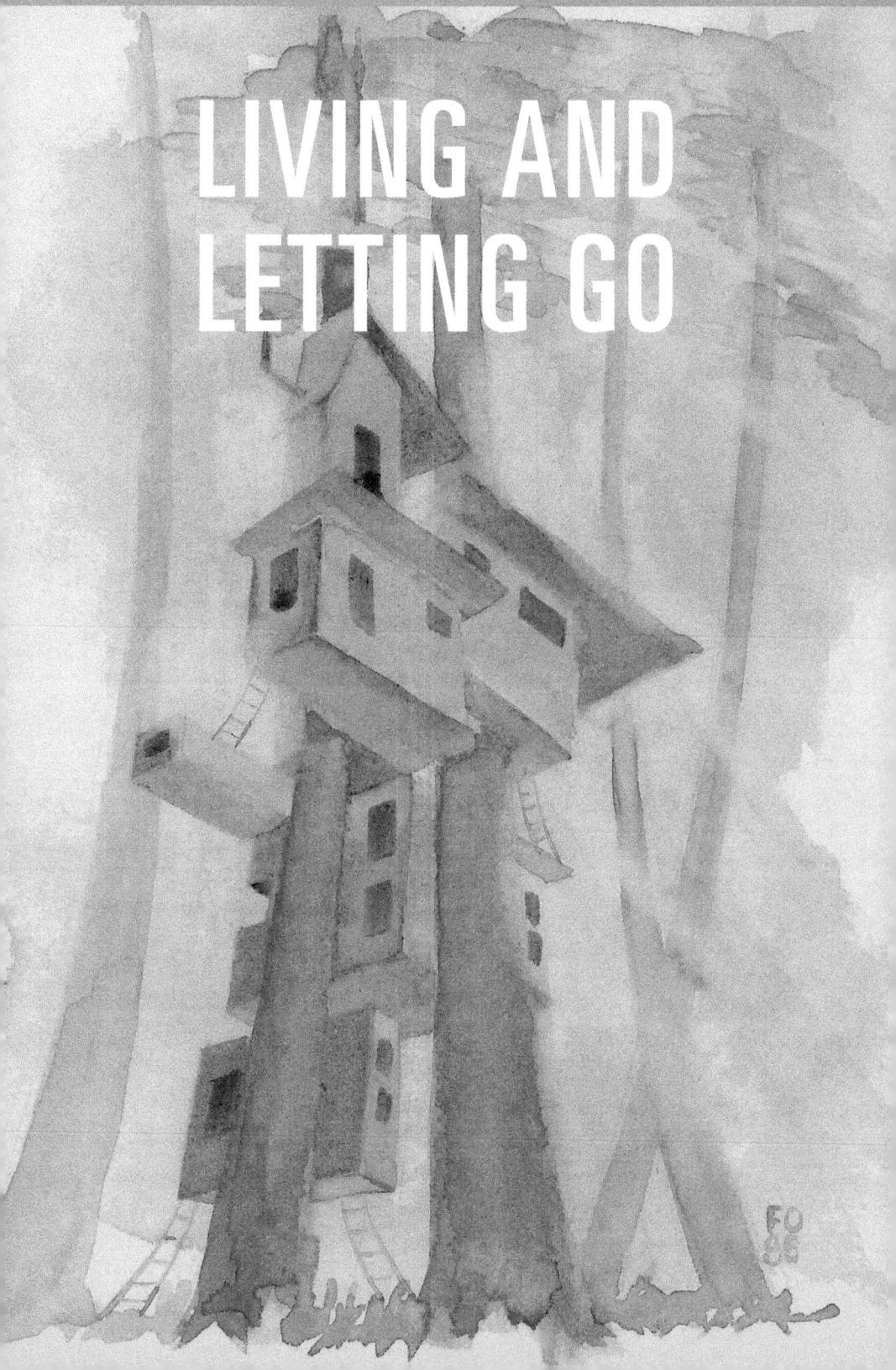

On Spirituality and Religion

Even before launching into this topic, I fully understand that bringing clarity to an issue of this magnitude is an extremely lofty idea. Over the years I have had countless opportunities to discuss, examine, and contemplate ideas associated with spiritualty and religion through conversations with patients and friends and through self-examination and reflection. I do not presume to know everything about these very complicated concepts, nor do I expect to present a complete understanding of all the different perspectives on these issues; however, I will nonetheless try to address what stands out in my thinking about them.

I have often pondered the place of spirituality and religion in a person's life. In some ways, the intensity of devotion and commitment to religion and spirituality appears to be stage (age) related. As young children and older individuals, we seem to embrace spirituality and religion with increasing forcefulness. Often in the years between young adulthood (ages 15–18) through approximately ages 55–60, we seem to be relatively less forceful and devoted in our attention to spirituality and religion. This set of generalizations is not intended to cover the entire population. Clearly there are people for whom spirituality and religion remain central throughout their entire lives without a drop of variance. However, I would like to propose that those people are somewhat of a minority, in particular with Judeo-Christian religions.

As a way to start, it would be helpful to differentiate spirituality and religion. While the concepts often overlap and admix, at least in people's minds, they may also be quite distinct. One way to think of religion in general is that it represents a set of laws, rules, regulations, and traditions that groups of people accept and utilize in order to unite with, communicate with, appeal to, beg forgiveness from, seek direction from, achieve absolution from, and gain protection from some more or less abstract conception of an all-powerful, all-knowing, all-seeing, idealized "other-worldly" object or objects. The anthropomorphism of this conceptual object(s) into a human form enables us to more easily relate to the specific object(s) of our religious practices.

While it is not overtly stated or demanded as a prerequisite for being a "religious person," it may be that devotion to the "other," the higher being, and the abandonment of certain aspects of the "self" facilitate the process of religious attachment and fulfillment. That is absolutely not to say that there is no significant self-soothing, self-gratification, and enhanced self-esteem derived from adhering to a set of religious principles, and from seeing oneself as a "god-fearing" individual. When you consider what most people believe about themselves and their relationship to their particular deity, the idea of "god-fearing" is rather interesting. It seems to contradict, or at least complicate, the idea of a loving, benign, magnanimous, forgiving, absolving god.

And while I am not specifically differentiating among the many religions of the world, the concept of devotion and connection to a powerful omnipotent, life-influencing "image" lies at the center of all religious belief. At the very least, one's personalized connection to that conceptual figure is at the very core of religious thought, even though that connection may express itself in myriad ways and may engender a widely disparate set of internal feelings in the believer, regardless of the specific religion. I believe that the subjective experience of communication and connection with that object is the feeling that believers seek and cherish, and from which they gain longed-for self-soothing, personal meaning, and feelings of self-empowerment.

At the point of "connection with the other," the concept of spirituality enters the mix. One way to think of spirituality is as a feeling or perception, nebulous and non-specific though it may be, of a union (connection, contact, commonality) with oneself, with others close to us, and with the world (cosmos) in general. Said another way, through empathetic and intimate contact with ourselves and with others around us, we develop a feeling of commonality, sharing, understanding, and community that supersedes the importance of our individual selves. "Feeling spiritual" is about ongoing and personal contact with the workings of your inner self and about a feeling of connection to your personal world and its meaning. The intimate connection between your own inner self and the inner selves of others may well be the height of spiritual experience.

The major distinguishing factor between spirituality and religion is that in spirituality the connection is primarily to oneself; from that intimate knowledge of self, one can springboard into deep and intimate connection with the selves of others. In religion, the primary connection is to the "other." Both spirituality and religion, albeit in different ways, yield self-soothing, personal empowerment, and potential for enhanced self-esteem and feelings of value in one's world.

In an early treatise, Sigmund Freud considered people's adherence to religion and religious precepts to be based upon an acceptance of a permanent infantile position. Unfortunately, because this can be seen as a pejorative comment, without more complicated explication, much of what he had to say regarding underlying or unconscious issues involved in religion were not seriously enough considered or welcomed. In fact, this may be one of the major contributing factors as to why the pathways of psychoanalytic thought and religious thought have largely parted company.

Freud's hypotheses essentially suggest that religion as motivation for the intense connection between the individual and some omnipotent figure is the "reincarnation" or unconscious continuation of one's archaic parent-child relationship, and that the connection to a god-like object psychologically resembles or imitates the child's earlier relationship to the all-knowing, all-seeing, all-powerful parent. Similar to the young child who attributes all power and control in the universe to the idealized parent, the religious individual's connection to the concept of god exactly mirrors that relationship. And like the child who turns to his idealized parent for protection, direction, absolution, praise, and role-modeling, the believer has allowed an unconscious transfer of authority to a god-like figure in a sophisticated repetition of that earlier parent-child relationship.

I think of a story I heard from a patient some years back, a story with some poignancy and directly related to the topic at hand. He reported that as an adult he would repeatedly experience a familiar set of feelings each time he would enter a synagogue on Jewish High Holy Days, and at other times as well, but particularly on those holiest days in the Jewish calendar. Immediately upon entrance into the synagogue he would be beset with a pervasive feeling of sadness and longing, and he could not attribute the feeling to anything consciously available to him. He might have been feeling quite upbeat and balanced upon leaving home, but the minute he was in the synagogue he would feel an overwhelming sense of loss and sometimes even intense, unexpected tearfulness.

Over the course of our work together, he uncovered certain memories that helped him understand and eventually work through these instances of seemingly inexplicable sadness. The critical memories were derived from his early childhood. He recalled that he would regularly spend weekends with his maternal grandparents, and as part of the weekend schedule he would accompany his grandfather to their local synagogue on Saturday mornings. He would sit beside his grandfather throughout the entire morning prayer service, feeling close, warm, and protected. His memory was of his grandfather having his arm around him, and he felt a strong, comforting sense that no harm could ever befall him in that setting, particularly because he was under the watchful and loving eye of his grandfather. And the feeling of closeness and connection to the grandfather was most intense (at least in his memory) in the synagogue.

There were times after the grandfather's death when he would return over and over again to that religious setting, but he could not "locate" that feeling of warmth and protection he had known earlier at his grandfather's side. Instead, what he felt was a sense of loss and disconnection, which precipitated tearfulness. One can see that his repeatedly returning to that setting in search of the feelings of comfort and connection might well have been confused with a deep feeling of religiosity and devotion (even by him). He was seeking the feeling that originally emanated from his memory of experiences with his grandfather, but of course the grandfather's absence in the synagogue now left him struggling with loss rather than with connection.

If one can accept that the intensity of the relationship to one's god(s) is based at least partly on the quality of one's relationship to the earliest, powerful, protecting, praising, directing, omniscient, idealized parental objects, then a careful exploration of those early involvements may well uncover insights into the nature and meanings of the relationships to the object(s) of a person's religious goals. To a large extent, the early connection to the idealized, omnipotent parental objects, and how that idealization is eventually managed in the parent-child relationship, will have major impact on the tendency to lean toward religious devotion and to find solace and empowerment in the connection to a god-like representation.

Optimally, the idealized parent-child relationship resolves itself with the gradual empowerment of the child through a slow and phase-appropriate giving up (by the child) of the perception that all power resides only in the parents and not in the child. This is the ideal process by which the former grandiosity attributed to the parents is resolved. An ideal end to this process is that the child feels her own empowerment without a devastating sense of disappointment and disillusionment in the face of the parents' inevitable shortcomings. Rather than being disappointed and disillusioned, and perhaps needing to desperately look for other objects to idealize (as substitutes for the now "fallen" parents) and from whom to seek direction and protection, the child will feel her own self-sufficient, self-directing, self-protecting, self-regulating core. And all of this ideally occurs under the loving and approving eyes of the parents.

Theoretically, the child who has neutralized the grandiosity she formerly attributed to the parents or other powerful authorities of childhood in a slow, non-traumatic way will turn less frequently to religion for solace and comfort. She will be confident about finding self-soothing and self-empowerment from within rather than seeking it in the connection to the outside "other."

Particularly in situations where there has been sudden disappointment and de-idealization of the parents or other guiding authorities, the child may feel a serious and compulsive need to replace the lost idealized object. Turning to religion and to a god that one can easily communicate with becomes a ready resolution to this quest. Alternatively, when parents maintain the position of ultimate and limitless power over the child long after it was time to begin transferring the power to the child, that child may also feel a desperate need to become empowered in some alternate manner. One thing is certain: the power does not reside reliably within him. Therefore, not only might he run from the overpowering parents, but he may also feel a strong need to attach himself to a powerful outside "other." This could be achieved either through emotional attachment to other charismatic and idealized people in his universe, or to an idealized, omnipotent god. This child may never feel personally powerful; he will feel empowered only through his closeness or attachment to some outside force.

The children who have experienced an optimal transfer of power between themselves and the idealized parents of their youth will maintain a strong connection with those parents in a balanced and mutual manner. And these children will most likely be able to get in touch with their spiritual side. They will not fear looking inside, nor fear seeing what exists in the core of their personality. Rather than hiding from their "center," they will be more curious and exploratory of what motivates and drives them and will pursue intimate connections with other similar-minded individuals. In fact, they will be drawn to the "center." They will embrace a spiritual feeling within themselves and will seek spiritual connection with others. After all, they are not afraid of themselves, nor are they afraid of closeness to other powerful people around them. Their self-sufficiency protects them and encourages connection and empathy with others.

As stated earlier, young children and older individuals appear to embrace religion more forcefully. Perhaps the personal perception of relative powerlessness (impotence) heightens and/or diminishes the unconscious need for intimate connection to the omnipotent other. The young adolescent brimming over with personal narcissism and feelings of invincibility will turn to the other far less willingly for direction or protection. Whereas the older person, worried about increasing loss of options, loss of personal power and personal influence, and perhaps even struggling with physical incapacity, may turn to the omnipotent other far more readily. The older person, feeling some loss of personal capability, may feel a greater need for protection, guidance, and help. Therefore, it is not a difficult jump to see why an omnipotent, protective figure might become more relevant and emergent in later life.

If one considers the dynamic of the transfer of power from the individual to some seemingly powerful, dynamic, energetic individual in the environment, and that this transfer of authority is based on a personal perception of heightening vulnerability of the self (whether accurate or not), it is clear why a charismatic, or even a messianic character type could emerge in such an environment. To the extent that people see themselves as weak and needy of protection and direction (albeit unconscious), they will be prepared to find such a character type to lead them. History is replete with such messianic and charismatic types. And depending on the goals and motivations of such individuals in leading their "flocks," the outcome can be constructive or massively destructive.

But it is not simply this need that drives people to return to religion more forcefully in later years. There is also a natural process of step-by-step transformation of personal narcissism and a feeling of self-importance, i.e., a sense of me at the center of my universe, into a feeling of cosmic narcissism, or of the greater relevance and importance of the world and its continuity, i.e., me and my personal narcissism at a much more peripheral place in my universe. The focus is increasingly upon the relevance and grandeur of the world (in particular on one's own specific and immediate world) and less and less on our own self-aggrandizement.

As the narcissism and grandiosity of our youth becomes either neutralized or transformed, we become more concerned with what has come before us and what will come after us; the absolute importance of our own being becomes far less central. The need to build statues to attest to our greatness is slowly replaced by a wish to facilitate the continuity of human kind. Thus, the wish to connect to others, to share experiences and knowledge and wisdom, and to be a part of a larger community supersedes personal aims and goals so staunchly held earlier in life. The return to religion, god(s), and spirituality is central to that increased wish for connection and sharing.

There is a glaring difference between the connection of the young child to her idealized world (including parents and other idealized figures) and the connection of the older individual to her now re-idealized world. In the latter instance, there is a far greater sense of "give-and-take" with the world. As an older person, much like the younger child, one receives emotional sustenance and nourishment from the world. But the older person also has much to give back, specifically in terms of personal experience, knowledge, wisdom, and understanding, all of which come from one's unique and idiosyncratic experiences through the years.

The young child's connection to her idealized world is primarily about passive receptivity, but for the older person her connection to her re-idealized world, while it also includes passive receptivity, now includes the potential for active, vitalizing, energizing generosity of spirit. This is a fundamental reward of aging: the ability to utilize one's experiences over time in order to enhance the well-being of those around you and to help create a supportive milieu for the generations to follow.

Reaching out to enrich those important people around us is spiritual connection at its finest. To prepare and inform them of what one can reasonably expect of the future and to alert them to potential traps is to make a spiritual connection of utmost importance. To share of yourself is to be spiritual, and to be connected to an all-powerful "other" is to be religious. And the two are not mutually exclusive.

On the Extreme

Most of us are given to extreme positions at one time or another, by which I mean we present arguments on myriad topics that we are absolutely convinced are the truth, and it becomes extremely difficult to move us off our position. In fact, we are so convinced of the veracity of our position, that to hear any other perspective besides our own, or to eventually listen to another point of view, especially if it is in any way opposed to our own, feels virtually impossible. "How can they not see the truth of my perspective? It is so completely obvious to me! What is the matter with them? To be so confused and so off base must indicate a total lack of understanding about the truths of this particular issue."

There are a wide variety of issues that can elicit extreme positions: for example, discussions about religion, political preferences, money and power, attitudes toward the poor and homeless, feelings regarding racial differences, and treatment of other countries or foreigners, to name just a few. It is critically important that when we find ourselves taking extreme positions on any topic, or becoming reluctant to consider other alternatives to our own "certain" truths, we should immediately become suspicious of that rigidity and lack of openness in our thinking. Because when we are truly certain of a particular position we hold, there is no reason to resist processing new information that might enhance our firmly held convictions. Behind a lack of openness, vulnerability may be hidden.

But what vulnerability? When we obsessively cling to absolute truths, it is likely that unresolved conflicts exist at a deeper level of the mind, perhaps relating to painful feelings and memories, superficially associated with the very topic upon which we have taken such an extreme position. We do not wish to entertain other perspectives because they may weaken the strength of our position. These are usually defensive positions that we have buttressed with fierce rationalizations and intellectualizations, but they strongly belie the existence of confusion, anxiety, and pain at a deeper level. And we really do not want to look at those buried feelings!

However, it behooves us to uncover and examine underlying and unresolved conflicts, primarily because in taking positions that clearly reflect extremism, we potentially alienate others and isolate ourselves. Who wants to be in a discussion with someone who resists new information, or insists on his convictions, irrespective of substantive facts to the contrary? This is not an inviting situation for anyone. And similarly in the reverse, we do not wish to engage others who summarily reject our perspectives without careful consideration, simply because they are different from their own. This dynamic does not make for ideal friends, colleagues, or partners in any endeavor. In fact, quite to the contrary, it leads only to angry confrontation, disagreement, and disengagement.

The sense of vulnerability arises from the fear that if I let a fresh, illuminating idea in, perhaps my house of defense will come tumbling down. The ultimate fear lies in the potential to re-experience pain and anxiety associated with the unresolved conflicts with an overwhelming intensity. These conflicts have been buried and covered over with powerful rationalizations because they are perceived as potentially disruptive and traumatic in nature. The fear of becoming overwhelmed and over-stimulated, and perhaps unable to neutralize the intensity of affect, is often based upon a decision made many, many years earlier through the eyes of a child. If these conflicts are examined in the light of day, through adult eyes and understandings, they may not be nearly as frightening, overwhelming, or psychologically damaging as expected.

While we certainly cannot suggest this self-reflective approach to someone else displaying an extreme position, we are quite capable of suggesting it for ourselves. But without the recognition that extreme perspectives suggest hidden stress, we will be compulsively driven to stay with our positions, defending them way beyond reason.

Group functioning and groups in general tend to facilitate extreme positions. Almost by definition, group members must share commonly held ideas. Without those criteria, what reason is there for coming together? The tendency to join groups with shared perspectives is particularly inviting for individuals who are ambivalent about the strength of their own understandings. Groups tend to make insecure people feel more secure. A lack of an internally derived sense of security or some serious doubt about one's understanding often forces one to seek external affirmation and an externally derived solidification of one's ideas. But the cost can be a loss of independence because autonomous thought will threaten the cohesiveness of any group. Thus the trade-off, in some cases, is security for independence of thought.

Mobs and mob mentality exhibit this feature very clearly. The effective messianic character will take unbridled advantage of this tendency in his disciples. The more forceful and sure he is in his statements, the more his flock will mimic his ideas and feel more secure in their newly found understandings.

Dealing with individuals who tenaciously hold on to extreme positions will often be very frustrating. In order to have creative and constructive dialogue between any two individuals, there needs to be some "wiggle room" available for understanding, for partial change, and for compromise. It is these very attributes that are absent with holders of extreme positions and that make it so frustrating (and even maddening) to converse with them. The more forceful the counterargument to their statements, the more it will be interpreted as an attack upon the self, thereby liberating a more intense or even violent counter-counterargument. The end point is utter disaster, certainly with respect to conflict resolution. There are many political situations currently at hand in the world that exhibit this difficulty in resolving conflict, made that much worse by both parties rigidly adhering to extreme positions.

Extreme positions can also be found in an aging population, particularly related to the aging process itself. If aging is considered only as an end stage, with its major characteristic being that it is one step away from death, any attempt to change that concept may be met with great resistance. But if individuals can begin to understand that their extreme positions are based upon fear (i.e., fear of the unknown, fear that time will slide by even more quickly, that they will be left empty, alone, and frustrated), they may well be able to manage that fear through self-analysis and/or with external support. They may then alter that extreme position taken on solely to justify their feelings of pessimism and impotence to change. Fear, and especially of the unknown, demands exploration and explanation, whether the explanation is realistic or not, in order for the fear to be managed.

The preservation of homeostatic balance and the achievement of tranquility is of utmost importance when raw emotion such as fear, panic, loneliness, depression, and loss are close at hand. But with emotional support (from oneself and others), and through self-reflection and self-examination, these raw emotions can be more effectively put to rest, freeing one up for creative and constructive attitudes toward aging.

Formerly held extreme positions, nurtured by ongoing conflict, can be carried into later life as well. But if life transitions and transformations yield new sources of self-esteem and well-being, extremism of all types (e.g., opinions, activities, grudge-bearing, etc.) can be slowly modulated. If life in later years is pursued in a pleasurable, stimulating, and satisfying manner, then the need to cling to old entrenched positions may become available for examination and eventual modification.

Generally speaking, the more vulnerable the individuals remain, the more rigidly and tenaciously entrenched are their positions. However, the more positive aspect of this issue of extremism and aging is that unconscious psychological conflict has a way of "burning itself out" over time, even without extensive self-reflection. Thus, formerly held extreme views can be significantly modified, sometimes in a totally seamless manner.

On Illness

Illness, especially serious illness, is the great "wrecker and destroyer." Nothing can disrupt the very best laid plans more precipitously than the onset of illness, be it acute or chronic, short-term or long-term, physical or mental, serious or even non-serious illness. Illness of any kind requires time, energy, attention, and resources; coping with illness can burn through potential opportunities faster than a raging forest fire. And the worst aspect is that we can do precious little to guard against the onset of illness.

Sure, there are things we can do to protect our health, such as exercise, diet and weight control, taking prescribed medications in a compliant manner, being cognizant of nutritional issues, and reducing stress levels, but by and large we remain vulnerable to major illness no matter what precautions we take, and especially as we age. There are also lifestyle choices we can make prophylactically, such as avoiding smoking, excessive drinking, persistent exhaustion, persistent stress, unhealthy foods (excessively high-fat or high-carbohydrate diets), excessive sunlight in an exposed state, etc. But even these precautionary measures will not guarantee excellent health forever.

The idea that illness is a common visitor to the older person is no revelation. But how do we prepare for it and should we be preparing for it at all? And if illness does strike, how do we best manage its impact on the rest of our lives? The answers to these questions obviously will vary widely based upon the nature and severity of the illnesses that befall us. Firstly, one must be realistic and acknowledge that illness is something we will all inevitably face. And one day it will win. But just maybe we can have more input on the eventual outcome than we ordinarily assume.

The shock with which we react when first diagnosed with an illness may set the tone for future management of this particular illness, and illness in general. When illness is experienced as a very serious overwhelming, or even debilitating blow to the self-esteem (and it is important to note that illness is always assaultive to self-esteem to one degree or another), the amount of psychological resilience that is evoked will correlate to the effectiveness of the body's resistance and resilience. Because stress and tension diminish illness-fighting aspects of the human body, psychological imbalance can be harmful to an individual's capacity to fight off illness. So, a robust attitude toward illness and fighting illness when it does occur will ensure the best possible bodily response to whatever negative influences are affecting you.

To be sure, acute onset illnesses can ravage and overwhelm a person's resistance, psychological and physical, no matter how resilient one is. But it is also true that with many of the more common chronic illnesses, such as hypertension, diabetes, cardiac disease, gastro-intestinal disease, arthritis, back pain, etc., a robust attitude toward fighting illness will have a significant positive effect upon one's ability to ward off rapid deterioration and progression of illness. I do not mean to suggest that the progression of all illness is determined primarily by psychological attitude towards the malady, but it does have an important impact on aspects of getting better, especially when there are things that can be done by the sufferer to slow the progression of the illness. A positive mental attitude about oneself and about one's ability to fight illness will have a positive effect.

The ability to "fight illness" is determined earlier in life by experiences in which we are faced with serious adversity and by how we managed them. And who among us has been able to totally avoid such trials? Adversity in any shape or form, which could include physical or emotional struggles in addition to a whole host of other conceivable stressors, challenges our resourcefulness and our self-confidence.

The degree to which we feel we can overcome adversity in whatever form it should arise will be dramatically influenced by past experiences in which we faced similar or different stressors, and the manner in which we addressed these stressors. The more successful we were in dealing with them, the more confidence we will have in overcoming the current stress. To have seen yourself in action, fighting against some frightening or worrisome "adversary," and to have met that challenge effectively will have a long-lasting and powerful impact on our sense of resilience. To have been overwhelmed and rendered impotent in dealing with stressors in the past will leave one worried and fearful about the next challenge.

I recall one situation with particular clarity. This was a young individual for whom getting through professional school was crucially important, primarily because his father and his older brother were already in that same professional field, and it was always assumed that he too would follow in their footsteps. But because of significant and deeply buried psychological conflicts, he found himself unable to continue with his studies. He essentially became paralyzed in pursuing his studies, which necessitated his eventual withdrawal from school for a period of time. He became acutely depressed, which further inhibited his ability to return to school. The idea of transferring to another professional area of interest was almost unthinkable and would have been completely unacceptable to any of the family members, but most especially to the individual himself. Following some in-depth psychotherapy, during which he was able to explore and master some of these deeper, unconscious conflicts, he was able to return to school and ultimately finished his studies in the area. He has gone on to be a very successful practitioner in his specialized area of expertise.

This man's struggle with deep-seated emotional conflicts and his eventual mastery over them, at least to a level where he could resume his studies and continue in the practice of his profession, left him with a lasting feeling about himself for many years after the fact, a feeling of self-confidence and assurance that he could meet adversity, no matter what might come his way in the future. More recently, the same man encountered a life-threatening illness with remarkable counter-force and power. The illness is now in remission and has been for over five years.

To a large extent, the response of the human (often parental) environment to early challenges against adversity, either with praise, indifference, or criticism, will also affect one's general sense of strength in challenging situations. Well-supported children will feel stronger about the next challenge because they felt praised solely for their effort, even if perhaps on their last outing they were not so successful. And on the contrary, the successful fight against adversity that goes totally unnoticed or unheralded or perhaps even criticized will likely leave these individuals feeling weakened, despite their "victory" against the challenge.

Optimally supported children will carry a feeling of strength and resilience into each of their challenges, irrespective of the outcome. And the unsupported or criticized children will often carry a feeling of apprehension and self-doubt into difficult moments; they will not ever feel resilient or robust, even if they repeatedly meet challenges effectively and efficiently. Early self-perception is extremely crucial in establishing feelings of empowerment and resilience. This sense of resilience and versatility allows us to fight illness with energy and vigor later in life.

As mentioned above, stress reduction acts as a significant prophylaxis against illness. It is unquestioned in medical circles that stress and illness of any kind are intimately interconnected. There was a famous British study done some years ago in which older men who had recently lost their wives of many years but were otherwise healthy were closely monitored for newly acquired physical illness in the years immediately following their wives' deaths. It was found that those men whose wives had died and who were now living alone were at least three times more likely to suffer with minor and major illnesses in the years following the deaths than with their wives. In this study, the effect of acute stress was the major factor in differentiating between these two groups in terms of the development of illness. This is but one of the many studies that suggest a strong relationship between stress, tension, emotional conflict, and the development of illness. The explanation for the development of all psychosomatic illnesses is based upon this premise as well.

Thus, attention to stress reduction is critical in the aging population, particularly since we are entering a time period when illness is expected and inevitable. This is not to say that stress reduction isn't important all the way through our lives, but it is especially important in the later years. But how do we achieve this stress reduction? It is easily stated that we should "relax, take it easy," but such a state might be achieved only with great difficulty and effort. While some of us may enter our later years with techniques for stress reduction firmly in place, many of us do not.

As in so many other instances, the first and most important step is recognizing and identifying that indeed we are suffering with stress. And the earlier in life we become aware of this suffering, the better. Generally speaking, stress reduction occurs in two major ways. Firstly and decidedly, the most effective technique is to identify the sources of the stress, usually deeply hidden (although not always), and to alleviate those stressors by change—either external or internal change. Internal stressors are the most entrenched and most difficult to root out. It is primarily through patient, persistent self-reflection and self-exploration that we successfully contact the internal sources of our tension and discomfort.

When the source of the internal stress turns out to be in reaction to some external, environmental issue, then one can alter the creation of stress by altering the environment. But the external sources of tension are far less often the source of stress than internal sources, often buried and conflictual material. When stress reduction is elusive despite repeated attempts at change, then one must look for internal, undiscovered causes. When the process of stress reduction remains exceedingly difficult or continually fails, then professional consultation is strongly indicated.

It is also possible to reduce stress by alternate measures, distinct from the process of gaining understanding and mastery over psychological conflict, namely through activities that effectively, although not permanently, reduce stress levels. This category includes the kinds of activities we think of as supportive of stress reduction. Activities such as physical exercise, mental exercise, friendships and connections to others, heightened communication and exchange, independent endeavors like tennis, photography, creative writing, art, in-depth study of particular areas of intellectual interest, exploring new horizons through travel, reading, or other investigative techniques, and a whole host of other actions or activities are all well-recognized for effective stress reduction. These latter modes of stress reduction are available to all of us, except for those of us with health-related issues that preclude any or all of these actions. Even with serious physical or emotional illness, one can still explore new avenues for reducing stress, even without physical output. Physical output, however, tends to be the outlet many of us look to first.

The single most crucial factor that allows an individual to effectively manage illness of any kind is not having to do it alone. A supportive relationship, or if you are fortunate enough to have a support system made up of several individuals with whom your quirks and idiosyncrasies are well-known and accepted, will facilitate your mustering your best resources to fight illness. While even the very best support system will not necessarily protect you from the ravages of serious illness, it will nonetheless make the whole process more tolerable.

Even if it is a bit clichéd to say, I believe strongly that we should live every day as if it were our last, especially as we age, and even more so if we are suffering with chronic, serious, or even terminal disease. The degree to which we can focus more upon what we do every day to have some fun and bring ourselves some pleasure despite whatever discomfort we may be experiencing, and the degree to which we can reduce the focus upon how ill we are feeling from day to day, will determine the quality of our lives as we age. To maintain a desire for joy and pleasure whenever possible, even in the midst of physical and emotional pain, remains a sensible goal for us all.

On Last
Goodbyes

How many times have we all heard someone say these words after a loved one has died or said these words ourselves: "I wish I could have . . . before they died; I'd feel so much better"? People who make this statement will find themselves focusing for some time on what they could have or should have said or done, or what they felt was left incomplete at the time of the loved one's death. This is a common phenomenon, even when the surviving individual was extremely attentive, sensitive, and empathetic in his or her dealings with the departed one. I believe this feeling has very little to do with the specific quality of terminal care provided to the deceased by loved ones. At times it may well be true that something else could have been said or done, but those efforts would not likely have changed the outcome of the situation in a substantial way.

Focusing on last interactions is more a reflection of disappointment about a more diffuse issue than it is based upon a single moment, namely upon that last interaction and its perceived inadequacy. No matter how successful and engaged two people are in their relationship, or how satisfying the relationship has been over a protracted time period, there inevitably exist some areas of disagreement over one issue or another over the course of any relationship. And while those moments of disagreement or even acrimony may not characterize the scope or quality of the relationship, at the time when the future of that relationship no longer exists or comes to a startling halt, those past moments of friction, no matter how insignificant they may have been, suddenly take on greater relevance. The wish to have said or done something differently in order to ensure a peaceful feeling when thinking about the relationship with the deceased is based upon remembrances of those past disagreements or conflicts. They leave some persistent feeling of uneasiness.

Additionally, the wish to have done or said just one more thing at the end of the loved one's life subtly suggests a desire to do the one thing that none of us can ever do; namely to prolong the lost one's life in a meaningful and valuable manner. Even when we all agree that a suffering, terminally ill person is "better off" dying and ultimately relieved of her pain and suffering, there still can remain a lingering feeling of "if only we could have done something sooner or something different." This relates to the universal feelings we all experience when loved ones pass away: "If only I could have done something to save their life and let them go on living a life of quality and pleasure . . . obviously I have failed to do so."

Individuals who feel they have missed some opportunity to do or say something relevant before a loved one's death may experience a deep sense of guilt or shame about their inadequate interventions. But very likely this is more a displacement of feelings of guilt or shame from the deeper feelings associated with the inability to change the course of the person's dying process and from the acknowledgment of our impotence to do so. But guilt and shame may also be related to those inevitable memories of unresolved disharmony that come back to mind at the time of death. There will be no further possibility of resolving residual disputes, so the residua come into much higher relief in the survivor's mind.

Loss and anger go hand-in-hand in this context; actual loss provokes both hurt and anger. Although often perceived as unpalatable to be angry at the dead person for dying and leaving, anger is an absolutely appropriate feeling. Something important or precious has been taken away or lost without the survivor having any say in the matter. Survivors feel angry about losing the possibility of additional contact with the deceased, as well as any future pleasurable exchange. It is far more palatable to direct anger at one's self than at the deceased, thus we find or create reasons to be angry at ourselves, to justify the anger we clearly feel. We feel deserving of this anger; just look at what we failed to do to save our loved one's life!

On Inheritance

In America, perhaps more than anywhere else in the world, parents seem over-focused on what we will leave for our children when we die. Why this becomes such a prominent concern for some people as they age is interesting to me. To a certain degree, an excessive focus on money and financial buying power is a part of this focus on inheritance. Nonetheless, I believe it to be a genuine and altruistic wish (in general but not in every case) that our children, grandchildren, and other significant individuals in our lives share and enjoy the fruits of our good fortune and labor after we're gone. A generous inheritance can improve lifestyles and provide opportunities to pursue chosen interests. Financial opportunities may be provided to heirs not only through the passage of money, but also of other valuable items, such as art, jewelry, houses, family-held businesses, real estate holdings, etc.

Parenthetically, I strongly believe that the "inheritance" that our children and grandchildren will value and cherish the most is not money or financial power, but our wisdom, direction, love, support, understanding, patience, and curiosity about them. Hopefully, our children will have experienced and internalized these emotional gifts long before our deaths. A valuable legacy is one that lives on forever; accretion of understanding and positive feelings about the self will linger in our loved ones' memories and can have daily impact for the rest of their lives. Not that money and financial security do not have value; they clearly do, as long as they are kept in proper perspective with emotional inheritance.

How do we most effectively and empathetically structure the passage of material wealth to our inheritors following our deaths? Most of us, although with some discomfort at addressing the issue of death, will create wills and other testamentary documents to clearly delineate where we would like certain gifts to end up. Considerable thought and reflection should go into decisions about the allotment of one's estate (no matter how large or small); at the time when the allotments are actually divided up, we will no longer be there to explain, change, or justify the particular apportionment. Providing for inheritance is our final interaction with those with whom we have related for so many years. Therefore, it behooves each of us to do it as "right" as possible. This might include consultation with professionals and eventual trustees, but also with close friends, relatives, and perhaps even with future recipients of one's giving.

If you are committed to open and close communication during your life, why leave this final communication as a surprise that occurs after you can no longer respond to the reactions of others? If you have been committed to communication with others, then this issue too has great value, not just so the inheritors know what to expect, but also so they can participate in and understand your decision-making process.

Because inheritance carries a symbolic permanence, you must be sure it is fair and equitable, and that others can reflect positively upon your decisions. All too often, old and unresolved conflicts get acted out through wills and testaments. Inheritance is the deliverance of the last word; one becomes stuck forever in an irrevocable position.

As I mentioned earlier, the wish to be generous to one's inheritors and to make their lives easier is not always based on a truly altruistic motive. For individuals who have failed to successfully transform their personal narcissism, centered principally upon themselves and their best interests, the ability to give freely to others may be significantly hampered. That is, it would feel nearly impossible to give to others without active acknowledgement and gratitude from the recipients. Whereas individuals with transformed narcissism can give to others even anonymously with no psychological strings of any kind attached, individuals still clinging tenaciously to their narcissism will have great difficulty and resistance in doing so. Their generosity is more contingent upon a "return upon investment," primarily the acknowledgment of their largesse.

Such individuals may act out old, unresolved battles and long-held grudges in their final communication with others. Needless to say, this is to be avoided. The best check against that kind of irreparable damage is to have trusted friends or relatives review all plans you've made about inheritance. Unfortunately, the ferocious anger of an un-neutralized, wounded narcissist may override even the sage advice of trusted friends and advisors.

Wise financial advisors and estate attorneys often suggest that wills and testaments be reviewed regularly—certainly every few years—to be sure that decisions made years earlier still reflect the current wishes of the grantor. This can provide each of us with repeated opportunities for balancing and equilibrating subtle inequities that may exist but remain unnoticed. A final will is one document that leaves no room for error.

On Dying

Now this is a very tricky subject. But it doesn't need to be. It is generally accepted that most people are afraid of dying, at least to some extent, because we certainly don't look at or discuss this issue with much eagerness or consistency. Perhaps this is because the firsthand experience of death is such an unknown commodity. Because we don't know how, when, where, or under what kind of circumstances we will pass away, there remains considerable mystery about this event for us and for people close to us. The unknown aspects make it all the more difficult to grasp why the prospect of death bothers us so much. I find it hard to believe that all the avoidance is simply based upon fear of that final moment and what it may entail. I also find it hard to believe that death is difficult because we don't know "where we'll be" the moment after death, whether it is all over after that fateful moment.

My sense is that the fear of dying is more intimately tied to the loss of living than it is to the fear of actually dying. We fear the total disconnection from everything we know and value. We will not be here to experience the things we were interested in or to interact with the people we love and care about most in the world. Life will go on without us, and we will be permanently excluded. That feeling of loss is monumental. And so the anticipation of that loss is not easily addressed, if at all, and more often dealt with through considerable denial. After all, the transience of one's time on earth can feel quite disturbing. The idea that I will lose all opportunity to achieve, to interact, to feel joyous, to engage in happy moments, to see how things turn out later, and to participate in important family moments or world events intensifies the sense of loss. And it is permanent.

We have all had our experiences with death at earlier times; for example, through the loss of grandparents, older aunts and uncles, family members of friends, beloved pets, teachers from our past, idealized political figures, acts, etc. We have experienced their physical absence, even though they may appear in our daytime thoughts or in our dreams. Through these experiences we see how memories, even memories of close loved ones, fade fairly quickly. It is often difficult to recall important attributes of the lost ones not that long after their deaths. Of course, they are not totally forgotten, but they cease to be an integral part of our daily lives and are certainly absent from our daily interactions. And when the mind is not "pleasured" by a live connection with another person, it turns away almost automatically from that object, allowing the active feelings and hopes that involve interactions with that person to slip into less available areas of the mind. An object that does not provide some degree of pleasure will be increasingly repressed and placed out of immediate, conscious awareness.

So once I die, not only will I miss the day-to-day excitement and challenges of my life, but I will also be relegated to a less active part of my family's conscious thoughts. What a dramatic feeling of loss. I was important, at least to those people in my immediate sphere of influence, and now I have been placed in some dark and dusty corner of their minds. And it all happens so quickly.

When you consider how important it is to each of us to exert positive influence on those around us and to effect positive change in our immediate universe, and how much self-esteem we have achieved by taking on those activities, it becomes easier to understand why death and the immediate negative impact of death on our deeply held wishes for ourselves can cause such emotional upheaval in anticipation of that event. One can see that the more narcissistic and self-important one feels, the more difficult the ultimate, inevitable loss of centrality will be for that person. And the more one has examined and accepted the limits of our powers and effects on others, and has made some kind of peace with our eventual non-participation in the infinite history of the world, the less frightening and overwhelming will be the loss of living.

Because death ends our contact with the living world, at least as we know and experience it today, it is not surprising that people do not want to give up on life, no matter how old they may be. The critical aspect that determines the wish to live is the potential for pleasurable interchange and activity with the world around us. If one considers the issue of suicide, the suicidal act makes "sense" (to a certain degree) if you consider that the suicidal person feels that the world holds no possibility for deriving pleasure now or in the future. He is certain that no matter what he tries, he will continue to experience his world as a place of frustration and deprivation. Holding a firm conviction of the absolute truth of that perception, the suicidal person asks, "What is the point of living? What pleasures can realistically be derived from sticking around here any longer?" Unfortunately, decisions about the potential for deriving future pleasures in the world, in the mind of an actively suicidal individual, are made at a time when his psychological universe may be especially dismal and may not reflect that person's potential experiences in the world over the longer term. In dealing with an actively suicidal individual, holding out the world as a place of hope and promise can be experienced by the sufferer as nonsense or false optimism. Of course, if and when we encounter a person suffering in this way, we are each obligated to proclaim the value of life, even in the midst of great despair.

Another challenging aspect in contemplating death and dying is the process of helping someone else die. While this is never a situation we would choose for ourselves, most of us will be at least tangential-ly (if not centrally) involved in watching and helping another person through the process of dying. It is difficult to know precisely what our role ought to be. Clearly we do not want the dying person to fear death, and instead want him to understand as best he can the issues of departing life. We may or may not be given to direct and explicit discussion regarding these types of issues; however, it is critical that open interchange occurs during the process of dying, particularly if the dying person is lucid and capable of comprehending the issues involved.

Some might see this as a cruel and unnecessary set of conversations, yet dying people often feel relieved, understood, and more peaceful with the eventuality when open and honest dialogue has occurred. It is particularly comforting if the frank discussions have been with the most loved and cherished people in their lives. And the discussion needs to be about the relevant issues that arise from death and dying. The obvious issues include funeral arrangements, memorials, eulogies, burial sites, and other such final details. But the less obvious issues are even more important. This kind of discussion might include the dying one's feelings about giving up life and the loss of possibilities for the future. In this context, the individual can consider, "What will happen in the world after I'm gone? What will happen to those people most important to me? How will they be cared for?"

A sense that the world I leave behind is in reasonable order and that the things I can take care of have in fact been taken care of can be an enormous relief. And yet, unrequited wishes in the dying person's life can have a distinct place in those final discussions because they can serve as guiding lights for the generations that come afterward. The firm establishment, in the mind of the dying person, but also for those around him, of an ongoing connection to what transpires even after he is no longer here can offer great solace to all. Frank discussion of this sort is never intended to minimize the significance of the dying person. In fact, it is an opportunity to establish in a more lasting way the importance of that person to those who will survive him.

The possibility of an eventual re-connection or "meeting again" at some later time, whether conceived of as an after-life or other religious idea, can also bring enormous relief and comfort to the dying person and to those around him. This idea is highly effective, irrespective of specific religious beliefs. It assaults the very core of what is most fearful about death and dying, namely the separation from loved ones and the idea of endless isolation and exclusion.

As with any difficult or painful psychological issue or transition in one's life, meaningful discourse, especially among loved ones, will significantly diminish the anticipatory anxiety associated with change and facing the unknown. Unfortunately, like so many other aspects of the aging process, we sometimes assume that avoidance or denial of the reality will make it all go away. By avoiding open exploration of our fears of all the great unknowns in life, we facilitate a state of increasing (and unnecessary) tension and worry. Death is absolutely no different in this regard! Whenever possible, frank discussions about death and dying between the dying person and those most important to him or her, instead of being morbid or uncomfortable, will actually enhance a sense of peace for everyone involved.

On Wisdom

I consider the acquisition of wisdom to be the single most relevant and gratifying of all experiences that come to us later in life. It's not that a young person cannot be wise, quite to the contrary, but the kind of wisdom that comes slowly through living life and learning from personal experience takes time and maturation. It's not like one day you're not wise and the net day you are wise. The acquisition of wisdom is much like the acquisition of knowledge; we experience step-by-step accretions to our base of information.

Whereas knowledge can be seen as the accumulation of an ever-widening array of facts, wisdom is more based upon a deep understanding of the way things are and how they work, not necessarily a description of their essential make-up. This may only be a semantic or connotative difference, but wisdom feels like a more dynamic and energizing force, whereas knowledge is more absolute, quantifiable, and unemotional. And yet one can see areas of significant overlap between the two concepts. We could even consider wisdom to be "working knowledge."

Wisdom is acquired through experiential learning over time, but experience alone is not all that is required for wisdom. We need to engage in active mental and psychological processing of our experiences. Careful reflection upon the information we glean about our world and efforts to understand why this information is meaningful ultimately yield wisdom.

Wisdom without the capacity to articulate what has been processed and learned is still exceedingly worthwhile, but only to the person engaged in that process. For wisdom to carry its fullest value and deliver on its promise of utility, the bearer of wisdom must be capable of successfully communicating with others. To a certain degree having wisdom is like having empathy; unless you can communicate empathy to another person, it is not of much value.

Wisdom, like empathy, can be simplified into a two-step process. The first step is knowing. In wisdom, knowing occurs through a slow accumulation of experiences and reflection upon those experiences. In empathy, knowing is achieved through listening and sensitive intuition of what the other person is experiencing and the source of his or her emotions. But in both cases, a response needs to be made in order to complete the process. In empathy, one must formulate a response that communicates an intuitive understanding of the other's emotional moment, and through that understanding one shares the emotional feeling with the other. The effect of the empathetic response is to lighten the burden of an emotional reaction, particularly if it is painful in nature, and to communicate a shared understanding of the other's experience.

While it may not be essential for one's wisdom to be shared with the surrounding world, when one does choose to share wisdom with others it can enhance the experience of utility and generosity for the bearer of the wisdom and create new insights for the others. This is clearly a mutually beneficial and gratifying experience for both. The same is true of a shared empathetic moment between two people. All parties in these shared interactions leave feeling "fuller." To miss or avoid the opportunities of sharing wisdom or empathy is to step away from heightened self-gratification and self-esteem.

Of course, individuals are equipped with varying capacities to communicate with others. And the style that we use to communicate also varies widely. Some will be natural teachers, others will be powerful historians and storytellers, others will use interaction to impart information, and still others will broaden understanding through facilitating a process of self-discovery for the people around them. Irrespective of the particular technique utilized for communication or the subject about which we communicate, the sharing of wisdom is beneficial to all parties involved in the exchange.

It is a complicated question as to why two people who have gone through fairly similar life experiences will have such different capacities to understand or reflect upon their experiences and may therefore internalize widely varying impressions. It is not simply a matter of differing intellectual capacity, although that can have some significant impact in certain cases. But the larger issue relates to a person's ability and willingness to learn.

In order to learn effectively, one must have a number of characteristics that collectively lead to a willingness to learn. First, in order to learn from external sources, one must feel comfortable "not knowing" and "confessing" to not knowing. If life circumstances have created an individual who cannot feel comfortable in his own not knowing, then he will not be open to new information. A person who cannot be wrong without feeling great narcissistic assault will essentially close himself off to learning.

The manner in which we were first taught anything new and the degree of support and patience shown to us, especially when we failed at early attempts, will have tremendous bearing on our willingness to plead ignorance or to try new activities, be they physical or mental. If early learning of anything new occurred in an emotional vacuum, i.e., without appropriate emotional support and praise, learning activities later in life will trigger the lonely, disappointed, or even shameful feelings of childhood, and the person will shy away from learning challenges. If one's early experience of learning was isolating, frustrating, or overwhelming, or if one experienced undue criticism or a lack of empathetic understanding of the struggles sometimes associated with learning, then that person will not eagerly seek out knowledge or wisdom.

Unfortunately, people with such negative early learning experiences are often closed to discussion and new ideas. Any new concept becomes a challenge to their basic integrity and self-conception. Anything that threatens to change the internal infrastructure they have painstakingly created in order to feel protected from the inevitable and precipitous transitions in life will be studiously avoided. They might be experienced by others as rigid and inflexible thinkers, but rigidity and inflexibility are built on vulnerability. And while such a person may be difficult or infuriating to engage in a debate, there is nothing more painful to witness than an individual desperately trying to maintain his internal balance in the face of an obvious need for internal change.

In order to acquire wisdom, the capacity for open and unstructured learning and processing of new information is essential. In becoming wise, we are constantly in flux, constantly required to shift our understandings based upon what we have witnessed or experienced. If we cannot comfortably transform our cognitive infrastructures, then the acquisition of wisdom becomes a painful trial rather than a dynamic and enriching pursuit.

And what is it that we become wise about? The acquisition of wisdom is more an experience of active synthesis that comes from many objective and subjective observations, and less an experience of passive infusion of information. Wisdom is gained by sifting through a multitude of opinions and facts, finding the explanation(s) or solution(s) that best fits the particular situation. Wisdom is often based upon the processing of direct experience that the wise person has had, or upon his thoughts and ideas. We cannot know and experience everything, but we can learn to extrapolate from our own personal experiences to the ones we are trying to understand.

There is no simple formula for arriving at wisdom. It's about being open to new experience, to new learning, to step-by-step processing of what's been seen, felt, or heard in order to generate some non-specific feeling and sense of how it all fits together. One must be ever willing to reconsider and revise basic infrastructures and understandings. Acquiring wisdom is not like acquiring a new skill and then sharpening that skill through practice, like you would with photography, golf, or creative writing. Wisdom happens by the very nature of your personality and by the cognitive capacities you bring to your experiences. I don't think you can plan for wisdom, or search for wisdom, or reject it if it appears. To be wise is to accept with absolute clarity that what we know now is only the smallest glimpse into all that is knowable in our universe.

Index

Adversity—88–90

Aging—3–7, 12, 16, 18–21, 23, 24, 29, 31–35, 41, 44, 46, 47, 51, 52, 59–62, 65, 70, 80, 86, 91, 105

Anger—43, 49, 64, 95, 99

Awareness—3, 4, 7, 11, 14, 18, 19, 46, 69, 102

Bannister, Roger—19

Behavior—14–16, 33, 46, 47, 49, 53–55, 57, 58, 60, 64, 65, 69

Brady, Tom—17

Children—9–11, 13, 15, 21, 25, 41, 43, 45, 55, 60, 63, 67–69, 73, 78, 79, 90, 97, 98

Conversations with—68

Churchill, Winston—17

Connection—39–41, 43–45, 54, 58–60, 62, 65, 68, 74–81, 92, 102, 104

Creativity—10, 17, 27–29, 33, 65

Death—3, 62, 77, 86, 90, 91, 93, 94, 98, 101–105

Discovery—11, 27, 109

Dreams—21, 33, 62–64, 102

Dying—3, 12, 94, 95, 101, 103–105

Empathy—39, 46, 64, 68, 79, 108

Empathetic—75, 93, 108, 109

Unempathetic—40

Emerson, Ralph Waldo—45

Emotional gift—98

Exploration—7, 21, 22, 46, 54, 55, 77, 86, 91, 105

Extreme—57, 83–86

Family—4, 21, 25, 43–47, 50, 51, 89, 97, 102

Financial advisors—99

Freud, Sigmund—50, 75

Gates, Bill—17

Goals—10, 12, 15, 16, 18, 19, 27, 28, 32, 54, 63, 77, 79, 80

Grandchildren—41, 45, 63, 68–70, 97

Grandparenting—69

Happiness—15, 56

Harmony—28, 57, 94

Health—4, 32, 65, 87, 92

Humanity—28, 30

Illness—4, 62, 63, 87, 88, 90–92

Inheritance—13, 97–99

Inner self—22, 75

Intimacy—40, 41, 57, 61

Joy—6, 14–16, 43, 55, 58, 60, 62, 63, 67, 69, 92

Knowing—14, 16, 34, 35, 39, 41, 62, 68, 74, 76, 108, 109

Later life—7, 16, 18, 24, 35, 56, 60, 63, 79, 86

Living—6, 12–14, 29, 53, 63, 90, 94, 101, 103, 107

Loss—3, 4, 6, 23, 25, 32, 34, 49, 65, 76, 77, 79, 85, 86, 95, 101–104

Love—15, 16, 21, 35, 53, 64, 65, 68, 97, 101

Marriage—61–63, 65

Maturity—34

Narcissism—47, 48, 54, 57, 58, 64, 70, 79, 80, 99
    Cosmic—47, 48, 70, 80
    Personal—47, 54, 70, 79, 80
Narcissistic—47, 49, 54, 103, 109

Openness—57, 83, 84

Peace—50, 52, 103, 105
    In the valley—52
Productivity—7, 10–12, 17, 23, 27, 28

Questions—4, 12, 30, 88

Reflection—5, 7, 14, 21, 33, 35, 40, 42, 62, 73, 86, 91, 93, 98, 107, 108

Relationships—39–41, 50, 59–65, 77

Religion—73–75, 78–80, 83

Retirement—6, 7, 23–25, 45, 46

Rilke, Rainer Maria—64

Roosevelt, Eleanor—17

Self-analysis—33, 86

Self-esteem—4, 11, 12, 19, 20, 23–25, 29, 32–34, 39, 40, 46, 47, 51, 56–58, 63, 74, 75, 86, 88, 102, 108

Self-exploration—7, 21, 46, 91

Self-reflection—7, 33, 35, 62, 86, 91

Sexuality—53–60

Spirituality—73–75, 80

Stress—12, 23, 25, 34, 62–65, 85, 87–92

Success—3, 12, 15, 17–19, 22,
    33, 34, 63
Suffering—40, 91, 92, 94, 103
Support—4, 25, 26, 45, 47, 61,
    63, 65, 86, 92, 97, 109

Time—3–7, 9–13, 15, 16,
    19–23, 27, 29, 32–35, 39, 41,
    44–48, 51–53, 55, 58, 60,
    62–65, 67–69, 76–78, 80, 83,
    86, 87, 89, 91, 93, 94, 98,
    102–104, 107
Time management—7, 9, 10, 41
Trauma—33, 34

Van Gogh, Vincent—28
Vitality—30

Will—98, 99
Wisdom—5, 80, 97, 107–111

Youth—5, 21, 31–33, 35, 78, 80
Youthfulness—31–33

About the Author

Leonard D. Elkun, M.D., is a psychoanalyst and psychiatrist who has been in private practice since 1972. He has treated a great many individuals of all ages, and has addressed a variety of different areas of focus within the field of psychiatry.

After finishing a residency in psychiatry at the University of Chicago in 1970, and spending two years on staff in the Department of Psychiatry at the University, he began his private practice and has been active in that endeavor since then. In 1970 he began psychoanalytic training at the Chicago Institute for Psychoanalysis, completing that in 1976.

He has worked in drug addiction facilities in the Chicago area for many years and has also spent time treating eating disorders in a wide range of ages. Since 1993, he has worked with the geriatric population in assisted living facilities in Illinois, primarily in the treatment of dementia. He remains very active in dealing with medical-legal cases, having made the diagnosis and treatment of individuals suffering with Post-Traumatic Stress Disorder (PTSD), a major focus of his forensic work.

Throughout these different areas of focus, his main interest has always been in adult psychotherapy and psychoanalysis. He has brought the theories and strategies of those modes of treatment to his day-to-day work in each sphere of interest. Both psychiatric training and psychoanalytic thought have shaped his attitudes and understanding of the world.